Tax Planning Strategies

Tax Savings Opportunities
for Individuals and Families

2005-2006 Edition

CCH Editorial Staff Publication

CCH INCORPORATED
Chicago
A WoltersKluwer Company

Editorial Staff

Managing Editor: Linda O'Brien
Revision Editors: Glenn Borst, John Buchanan, David Jaffe
Production: Angela Cashmore, Kristine Jacobs, Don Torres
Cover Design: Don Torres

Tax Planning Strategies was previously published by
CCH INCORPORATED as *Year-End Tax Strategies*.

This publication is designed to provide accurate and authoritative information in regard to the subject matter covered. It is sold with the understanding that the publisher is not engaged in rendering legal, accounting, or other professional service. If legal advice or other expert assistance is required, the services of a competent professional person should be sought.

ISBN 0-8080-1351-3

© 2005, **CCH** INCORPORATED
4025 W. Peterson Ave.
Chicago, IL 60646-6085
1 800 248 3248
http://tax.cchgroup.com

Planning Opportunities for Now and the Future

During the past four years, Congress has passed several major tax relief packages aimed at boosting the economy and included tax benefits for both individuals and businesses. Beginning with the passage of the Economic Growth and Tax Relief Reconciliation Act of 2001, tax planning has been particularly challenging. Due to federal budget constraints, most tax breaks enacted in 2001 were only temporary and many were phased in over a number of years. Later, the Jobs and Growth Tax Relief Reconciliation Act of 2003, which followed the 2001 Act and the Jobs Creation and Worker Assistance Act of 2002, introduced a host of new tax breaks and accelerated benefits previously not set to take effect until 2006. The 2003 Act also created many retroactive phase-in/phase-out effective dates and provisions that were temporary in duration.

In 2004, Congress passed two tax bills shortly before adjourning for the November 2004 presidential election. The Working Families Tax Relief Act of 2004 focused primarily on providing tax relief to married taxpayers with children. Several individual tax cuts, originally due to expire in 2004, were extended. In addition, several business tax provisions that had already expired were retroactively extended through 2005. The American Jobs Creation Act of 2004 repealed the foreign sales corporation/extraterritorial income regime and created a new manufacturing deduction. Significant changes to S corporation rules were made, along with the extension of increased expensing and depreciation deductions for small businesses and a new state sales tax deduction for individuals.

The result is a revolving door of tax rate and other changes between now and 2010 that make mid- and long-term tax planning difficult and more tax-driven than ever before. Coupled with news of continuing economic uncertainty and financial downfalls, taxpayers are left to wonder what they can do to ease the tax bite on their financial situation. With so many provisions being temporary in nature and phased in and phased out over the next decade, tax planning is essential to maximize many of these benefits.

A handy Quick Tax Facts chart contained in this publication provides an at-a-glance reference for key tax figures and outlines a 10-year forecast of important amounts and percentages impacted by the phase-in and phase-out dates from the legislation discussed above.

With change comes opportunity, and the recent tax relief packages have created an environment in which taxpayers can choose among a number of options to invest more and deduct more, all while paying less in taxes. The reality of across-the-board tax rate cuts guarantees lower tax liabilities for almost everyone, but there are so many additional aspects lurking that proper tax planning takes on a more critical and valuable role. Individuals have more options for retirement savings, families have more ways to finance education, and estate planning has taken on a life of its own. However, to best maximize tax savings, you must keep in mind which tax breaks are scheduled to expire and which ones have already expired. Finally, added to the mix is the realization that future tax legislation will likely further complicate the planning landscape.

Whether working with a professional advisor or planning on your own, effective and efficient tax planning is now much more than a year-end task to defer some income while accelerating a few expenses. The current economic conditions have raised the stakes for tax planning, and doing nothing can be the worst course of action that one can take. In response, this book, previously published in annual editions as *Year-End Tax Strategies*, has been revised to reflect year-round tax planning strategies.

This publication is designed to provide information and insight to help you make the right tax planning decisions. "Tax Alerts" and "Legislation Highlights" point out changes from recent tax legislation, while "Planning Alerts" and "Tax Tips" are provided throughout for additional practical information. Beyond the comprehensive discussions of assorted tax planning topics and strategies, in addition to a Quick Tax Facts chart, the publication includes the 2005 individual income tax rates, an average itemized deduction chart, a deductions checklist and a 2005/2006 tax calendar.

June 2005

TABLE OF CONTENTS

CHAPTER 1: IMPORTANCE OF TAX PLANNING

Using Tax Rate Differences 10
Understanding the AMT 12

CHAPTER 2: INCOME SUBJECT TO TAX

Common Types of Taxable Income 15
Excluded Income 16
Social Security Benefits Taxed 17
Reducing Tax on Social Security Benefits 17
Shifting Income 18
Ways to Postpone Income 18
Ways to Accelerate Income 21
Taking Advantage of Flexible Spending Accounts 22
Avoiding the Risks of Incentive Stock Options 23

CHAPTER 3: MAKING YOUR DEDUCTIONS COUNT

Maximizing the Value of Itemized Deductions 28
Avoiding the 2% Trap of Miscellaneous Itemized Deductions 31
Minimizing the Effect of 7.5% AGI Floor on Medical Expenses 32
Additional Medical Expense Planning 33
Multi-Year Planning for AMT 34
Qualifying for Deductions 35
Maximize Your Charitable Contribution Deduction 36
Try to Collect on Debts 37
Protect Your Business Expense Deductions 37
Accelerate Depreciation on Your Business Assets 38
Expensing Business Assets Under Code Sec. 179 40
Seller-Paid Points—A Deduction for Home Buyers 41
Benefits of Renting Your Vacation Home 41

CHAPTER 4: INVESTMENT DECISIONS

Determining Holding Period 44
Capital Losses 44
Worthless Securities 45
Planning Your Investment Transactions 46
Dividend Income 47
Shifting Capital Gains Tax Through Gifts 49
Capital Gains and Inherited Property 50
Additional Capital Gains Considerations 50
Timing Decisions 52
Wash Sales 53
Mutual Funds: Recordkeeping Is Key 54
Investment in Qualified Small Businesses 55
Investment in Small Business Investment Companies 56

Tax-Exempt Bonds 57
Sale of Principal Residence 58
Sale of Vacation Home 60

CHAPTER 5: RETIREMENT PLANNING

Before You Retire 61
After You Retire 63
Benefiting from IRAs 64
Roth IRAs 66
Contribution and Deferral Limitations 67
Rollovers from Traditional IRAs to Roth IRAs 68
Keogh Plans 69
Employer-Sponsored Plans 69
Deemed IRAs 71
Inherited Retirement Accounts 71
Social Security Benefits 72
Estimation of Benefits 73

CHAPTER 6: EARLY RETIREMENT
AND POST-RETIREMENT STRATEGIES

Planning for Early Retirement 75
Social Security Benefits 76
Retirement Accounts 77
Medical Benefits 77
Estimated Tax Liability 77
Liquidation of Assets 78
Loan Qualification 78
Post-Retirement Planning 78
Asset Protection 78
Asset Management and Allocation 80
Long-Term Health Care 80
Incapacity 81
Housing 82

CHAPTER 7: ESTATE PLANNING—MINIMIZING ESTATE
AND GIFT TAXES

Estate Tax Exclusion 83
Marital Deduction 84
Lifetime Gift Tax Exclusion 84
Make Use of the Annual Gift Tax Exclusion 85
Educational or Medical Expense Exclusion 85
Gift and Estate Tax Rates 86
Stepped-Up Basis Rule 86
State Death Taxes 88
Generation-Skipping Transfer Tax 88

CHAPTER 8: FAMILY STRATEGIES

Shifting Income to Your Kids 89
Protecting Dependency Exemptions.. 90
Multiple Support Agreements 92
Dependency Exemptions of Divorced Parents 93
Adoption Expenses 93
Child Tax Credit.. 94
The Marriage Penalty 94
Child and Dependent Care Credit.. 95
Education Incentives.. 96
Education Tax Credits.. 96
Coverdell Education Savings Accounts 98
IRA Education Expense Withdrawals.. 99
Education Loan Interest Deduction... 99
Deduction for Higher Education Expenses.................................. 100
Qualified Tuition Programs 101
Employer's Educational Assistance Program 102
Exclusion for U.S. Savings Bond Interest.................................... 103

CHAPTER 9: ESTIMATED TAX

Do You Have to Pay Estimated Taxes?... 105
Safe Harbors 106
High-Income Taxpayers 106
Avoiding the Penalties 106

CHAPTER 10: BUSINESS PLANNING

Choosing the Right Business Organization................................... 109
Accounting Periods and Methods 113
Start-Up Costs 114
Retirement Planning as Business Owner 115
Employing Family Members... 116

CHAPTER 11: TAX STRATEGIES FOR THE SELF-EMPLOYED

Medical Expenses..117
Automobiles 121
Buy vs. Lease 121
Standard Mileage vs. Actual Costs 122
Vehicle Depreciation.. 122
Substantiation.. 124
Travel and Entertainment 125
Moving Expenses 125
Travel Away from Home.. 126
Meals and Entertainment... 127
Home Office... 128
Retirement Plans.. 130

Simplified Employee Pensions (SEP) 130
Keogh Plans 131
Savings Incentive Match Plan for Employees (SIMPLE) 132
Individual Retirement Account (IRA) 132
Taxation 133
Self-Employment Tax 133
Alternative Minimum Tax (AMT) 134
Employee v. Independent Contractor 134

CHAPTER 12: INTERNATIONAL TAX PLANNING

Overview of U.S. Jurisdiction 139
Sourcing Rules 140
Income of Foreign Persons and Entities 141
Foreign Earned Income and Housing Exclusion 143
Making the Move Abroad 145

APPENDICES

Appendix A: Tax Planning Checklist 147
Appendix B: Tax Calendar 150
Appendix C: Income Tax Rates 151
Appendix D: Average Itemized Deduction Chart 153
Appendix E: Deductions Checklist 154
Appendix F: Tax Items Affected by AGI 156
INDEX 159

Introduction
Importance of Tax Planning

Tax planning activities may often result in substantial tax savings. If you compute your federal income tax on a calendar-year basis, as most individuals do, your opportunity for tax planning generally ends on December 31. Thus, when you prepare your tax return two or three months after the close of the tax year, it is generally too late to do anything except file your return on the basis of what took place in the preceding year. There are some exceptions. For example, many individuals can make post-year-end IRA or Keogh plan contributions and reduce their taxes for the prior year.

Tax planning primarily concerns the timing and the method by which your income is reported and your deductions and credits are claimed. The basic strategy for tax planning is to time your income so that it will be taxed at a lower rate and to time your deductible expenses so that they may be claimed in years when you are in a higher tax bracket. This usually means that, if you expect to be in a lower tax bracket in 2006 compared to 2005, you should defer the receipt of income to 2006 and accelerate your deductions into 2005. Conversely, if you expect to be in a higher bracket in 2006, you should accelerate your income into 2005 and defer your deductions until 2006.

Here's an example of how the timing of income strategy works:

Let's say you and your spouse are both over age 60 and have been retired for several years. Your house is paid for and you've been living on savings and Social Security. You expect your taxable income for 2004 and 2005 to be $18,375 for each year. Near the end of 2004, you decided that you wanted to withdraw $50,000 from a traditional IRA in order to pay for major home improvements as well as paying off some of your high-interest credit card debt. Should you have made the withdrawal in 2004 or waited until 2005?

Neither. The correct timing strategy is to allocate the amount of the IRA withdrawal between 2004 and 2005.

For 2004, the withdrawal should be $39,725, which will be taxed at 15%. (For joint filers in 2004, $58,100 is the top end of the 15% tax bracket; $39,725 + $18,375 = $58,100.) The balance of $10,275 should be withdrawn after January 1, 2005, taking 2005 taxable income to $28,650 ($10,275 + $18,375). By splitting your IRA withdrawal between 2004 and 2005, and thus deferring some income until 2005, you will achieve an overall federal tax savings of $1,027 over what the liability would have been had the entire $50,000 been withdrawn in 2004. (Compared to the tax liability if the entire $50,000 had been withdrawn in 2005, the savings from splitting the withdrawal between the two years would be $897.) In addition, allocating your IRA distribution over two tax years accomplishes two other objectives:

- It makes maximum use of your lowest tax brackets (10% and 15%) for both years.
- It avoids, or postpones, the 25% tax bracket, giving you tax-free use of the money for a year.

Using Tax Rate Differences

We've given you the three cardinal rules of tax planning:

- Recognize income when your tax bracket is low.
- Pay deductible expenses when your tax bracket is high.
- Postpone tax whenever possible.

All these rules involve planning around your tax bracket. Your most direct control over your tax bracket rests in your ability to control the timing of your income and deductible expenses. However, you should also be aware of more indirect factors that act to change your tax bracket from one year to the next. These factors also present tax planning opportunities. Among these factors are:

Filing status. There are four schedules of tax rates that apply to individuals. Two apply to married persons and two to single persons. For married persons, the filing choices are "married filing jointly" and "married filing separately." In rare instances, a married couple may be able to reduce their overall tax liability by filing separate returns. If separate returns are filed, each spouse reports his or her own income and deductions on the return.

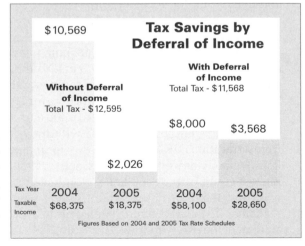

Tax Savings by Deferral of Income

$10,569

Without Deferral of Income
Total Tax - $12,595

With Deferral of Income
Total Tax - $11,568

$8,000

$3,568

$2,026

Tax Year	2004	2005	2004	2005
Taxable Income	$68,375	$18,375	$58,100	$28,650

Figures Based on 2004 and 2005 Tax Rate Schedules

Single persons must generally select "single" filing status. However, a single person who lives with and provides support for a dependent may file as "head-of-household." The head-of-household tax rates are more favorable than the rates that apply to "single" filers, but less favorable than those that apply to "married persons filing jointly."

In 2005, each tax rate schedule has six rates (i.e., 10%, 15%, 25%, 28%, 33%, and 35%) but the income level at which these rates apply will depend on the taxpayer's filing status.

The tax rate schedules for 2005 for each filing status are located in Appendix C at the end of this book. Remember, for tax purposes, your *marital* status is determined on the last day of the year.

Income level. The biggest variable determining your marginal tax rate is your income level, so big changes in income from this year to the next may open the door to several tax planning opportunities. Marriage and divorce often have a drastic effect on your income level, as do job changes, retirement, illness, cash windfalls, and sales of assets (e.g., stocks, mutual funds, or your home).

"Preference" items. Just when you think you have beaten the tax system by maximizing your itemized deductions and/or making the most of other tax breaks, you may find that the alternative minimum tax (AMT) has ruined your plans. The AMT system is in place to ensure that you pay a minimum level of tax. Thus, if your deductions are too high and/or you've taken advantage of too many other tax breaks, some or all of these "preferences" may be disregarded or modified in the AMT calculation. While the alternative tax is a burden, it also is a planning opportunity, particularly if you are subject to the AMT in one year but not in the next (or vice versa). The actual computation of an individual's alternative minimum tax is completed on Form 6251, "Alternative Minimum Tax-Individuals," and it is usually a very complex task. At this point, the important thing for you to know is that if you have a large amount of deductions or other preferences, you may be liable for the alternative minimum tax. If you are liable for this tax, you may be in a higher tax bracket than you thought. Because of this, the possibility of an AMT liability must play a role in your yearly tax planning.

 Tax Alert The Jobs and Growth Tax Relief Reconciliation Act of 2003 (P.L. 108-27), contained major tax cuts for individual and business taxpayers. The 2003 Act accelerated the reduced individual tax rates which were scheduled by the Economic Growth and Tax Relief Reconciliation Act of 2001 (EGTRRA) (P.L. 107-16) to take effect in 2006. The following chart shows the applicable tax rates.

2003-2010	10%	15%	25%	28%	33%	35%
2011 and later	N/A	15%	28%	31%	36%	39.6%

The 2005 Tax Rate Schedules which incorporate these brackets are reproduced in Appendix C. The taxable income level at which the brackets begin and end are adjusted annually for inflation. The 10-percent bracket will also be adjusted annually for inflation through 2010.

For 2005, the 10-percent bracket applies to the first $7,300 of taxable income for persons claiming single filing status or married filing separately filing status; the first $14,600 of taxable income for married taxpayers filing jointly; and the first $10,450 of taxable income for heads of households. (These are the base amounts subject to inflation adjustments through 2010.)

All of the rate reductions under JGTRRA were retroactive to January 1, 2003, and remain subject to the sunset provisions under EGTRRA. Consequently, the rates will revert to 15%, 28%, 31%, 36% and 39.6% after 2010 unless Congress takes legislative action.

A chart outlining 10 years of changes for the tax rates and other items is provided on the last two pages of this publication.

Understanding the AMT

Since the AMT system is not adjusted for inflation, record numbers of taxpayers, including a growing number of middle-income taxpayers, have paid this special tax in recent years. The Joint Committee on Taxation estimates that the number of taxpayers subject to the AMT will grow from about 1 million taxpayers in 2000 to more than 17 million in 2010.

By reducing your regular tax liability, the rate reductions enacted in 2003 may have triggered or increased your AMT liability. You are subject to the AMT if your tentative alternative minimum tax liability exceeds your regular tax liability.

Tentative alternative minimum tax liability is equal to: (1) 26 percent of the first $175,000 ($87,500 for a married taxpayer filing a separate return) of alternative minimum taxable income (AMTI) in excess of an exemption amount, plus (2) 28 percent of remaining AMTI.

For some persons subject to the AMT, the benefit of the 2003 rate reductions may simply have been delayed. This is because AMT liability may usually be claimed as a credit against regular income tax in years in which there is no AMT liability. The credit, however, is limited to the amount that the regular tax liability exceeds the tentative minimum tax liability.

For 2004 and 2005, the exemption amounts are:

- $58,000 for married individuals filing a joint return, and surviving spouses;
- $40,250 for unmarried individuals; and
- $29,000 for married individuals filing separate returns.

Tax Alert Without future Congressional action, the AMT exemption amounts for 2006 will return to those in place in 2000, namely $45,000 for joint filers, $33,750 for unmarried individuals, and $22,500 for married individuals filing separate returns.

Planning Alert For taxpayers subject to AMT, the full benefit of the nonrefundable tax credits may be denied.

For 2002 through 2005, the nonrefundable personal credits could offset both the regular tax liability and the AMT. However, after 2005, only the adoption credit, the nonrefundable portion of the child credit, and the retirement savings contributions credit (which expires in 2006) will be permitted to be used to their fullest extent.

Income Subject to Tax

In order to make your tax planning effective, you must have an accurate picture of your tax situation, not only for 2005 but also for 2006. The first step is to determine the amount of taxable income.

As a general rule, you are required to report and pay tax on all income "from whatever source derived." Income is gain derived from your labor and/or capital. The form in which you receive the income is irrelevant. It is taxable whether received as cash, services, meals, accommodations, stock, or other property.

Common Types of Taxable Income

The most common type of income is the compensation you receive in the course of your employment. This may be in the form of wages, salary, fees, commissions, or business profits. They are all taxable. Other common types of taxable income include:

(1) gains you receive on dealings in real estate, securities, and other property;

(2) interest you receive on bank accounts, CDs, securities and loans, etc.;

(3) rents you collect;

(4) dividends;

(5) royalties;

(6) alimony and separate maintenance payments you receive, if deductible by the payor;

(7) annuities and pensions;

(8) income from your share of an estate or trust, but not of any gift or bequest you receive;

(9) prizes and awards;

(10) certain fringe benefits; and

(11) for some taxpayers, up to 85% of their Social Security benefits.

This list is not exclusive. Cash or property that you receive is includible income, unless it is specifically excluded by federal tax laws.

 Tax Tip Remember that if you purchase a zero-coupon bond or a Treasury Inflation-Protected Security (TIP) and the bond is not held in a tax-deferred account (e.g., IRA), you must include the accrued interest in your income every year. This is true even though the interest or inflation adjustment is not paid to you until the bond reaches maturity. As a result, you don't reduce your current income by investing in these types of bonds.

Excluded Income

Certain types of income are exempt from tax. The following is a partial list of common types of items that are excluded from your taxable income:

(1) gifts and inheritances;

(2) interest on certain state, tribal and municipal bonds and interest received from mutual funds that hold such bonds;

(3) returns of capital (for example, loan principal repayments, the portion of the sales price of property up to your adjusted cost for the property, and the portion of annuity and pension payments that represent a return of your nondeductible investment);

(4) reimbursements you receive from your employer for business expenses;

(5) exclusion of up to $250,000 ($500,000 for married taxpayers filing jointly) in gain from the sale of your home;

(6) some or all of your Social Security benefits;

(7) compensation for injury or sickness, including worker's compensation and certain disability payments (but not wages or payments in lieu of wages under an employer plan or awards representing lost wages);

(8) employer-paid health coverage for you, your spouse and dependents;

(9) employer-provided education assistance;

(10) certain disaster relief payments; and

(11) qualified foster care payments.

Planning Alert Ministers may exclude from their church income the rental value of homes furnished by churches as part of their compensation. The exclusion covers rental allowances used by ministers to rent a home, to purchase a home, including furniture and utilities. The exclusion does not apply to the cost of food or for servants. Deductions for depreciation and repairs are not permitted.

Planning Alert States are generally prevented from taxing the retirement income of their former residents. Thus, if you receive retirement income and have moved from a state that imposes an income tax, your former state cannot tax the retirement income you receive while a resident of another state. The term "retirement income" is very broad and includes income from most types of pension and profit-sharing plans, IRAs, SEPs, and government retirement plans. In addition to individuals who are already retired, this bar to state taxation should play a part in the tax planning of individuals who are thinking about retiring and who want to move to a state with a "friendlier tax climate." In some situations, the savings on state income tax can be substantial.

Social Security Benefits Taxed

Social Security recipients may be taxed on a portion of their benefits if their income exceeds a certain amount. Individuals with lower income are taxed on up to 50% of their benefits or not at all. If your 2005 modified adjusted gross income exceeds $44,000 (for married filing jointly), $0 (for married filing separately), or $34,000 (for singles, heads of household and qualifying widow(ers) with a dependent child), then up to 85% of benefits must be included in your gross income.

However, if your 2005 modified adjusted gross income exceeds $32,000 but is not more than $44,000 (if you are married filing jointly), or exceeds $25,000 but is not more than $34,000 (if you file as single, head of household, or qualifying widow(er) with a dependent child), then "only" up to 50% of your benefits are taxed.

Reducing Tax on Social Security Benefits

There are a number of ways that Social Security recipients can reduce the tax bite on their benefits. For example, it may be possible to defer receipt of other income and thereby reduce the amount of benefits that will be taxed. For instance, a retiree may have a choice of receiving periodic pension payments or one lump-sum payment. By choosing the lump-sum and rolling it over into a traditional IRA, or other type of retirement plan, the funds will grow tax-free and won't cause a higher percentage of Social Security benefits to be taxed. By contrast, receiving pension payments each year would push up AGI and the amount of benefits subject to tax. Of course, a retiree must begin receiving distributions from a traditional IRA, and most types of retirement plans, by April 1 of the year after reaching age 70½. Many individuals will need to take distributions even before that age simply because they'll need the money. Other steps for reducing the tax bite on benefits include: (1) switching funds to EE bonds and/or I bonds, which permit deferral of interest until the bonds are redeemed, and (2) holding off on selling appreciated assets unless losses from other sales will be available to offset the gains.

Tax Tip Investing in municipal bonds will not help. While the interest from such bonds is not generally included in your gross income for federal income tax purposes, the interest must be included in your income when determining the amount of your Social Security benefits that are subject to tax. See page 57 for more information concerning tax-exempt bonds.

Planning Alert The Senior Citizens Freedom to Work Act of 2000 repealed the Social Security earnings limit as it applies to beneficiaries age 65 through 69. The repealed rule cut Social Security benefits of beneficiaries in this age bracket by $1 for every $3 earned in excess of a set "exempt" amount. Prior to passage of the Act, only retirees age 70 and above could earn unlimited amounts without a reduction in Social Security benefits. Taxpayers aged 65 to 69 who paid little or no tax on their limited benefits prior to repeal of the earnings limit may now be subject to tax as a result of receiving full benefits if their modified AGI is bumped above the applicable base amount. The law, however, does not affect the separate earnings limit for individuals who decide to begin collecting reduced Social Security benefits before reaching full retirement age. Your "full retirement age" depends upon your year of birth. For example, the full retirement age for an individual born in 1955, is when the individual reaches age 66 years and two months. See pages 72-73 for a chart that will show you your full retirement age.

Shifting Income

Shifting income from one year to another is one of the most effective techniques you can use to reduce your tax bill.

If you are like the vast majority of individuals, you calculate your taxes using the cash method of accounting. Under this method, income is taken into account when it is received and expenses are taken into account when paid. The cash method gives you a great deal of flexibility because income is taxed in the year you receive it rather than in the year you earn it.

Ways to Postpone Income

If your tax planning shows that you will be in the same or a lower tax bracket next year, you probably will want to delay the receipt of year-end income until early next year, provided the delay does not jeopardize your prospect of collecting the income. However, if the IRS feels the shift on receiving income was made to postpone income, you will be deemed to have received the income in the prior year. Here are a few techniques you may be able to use to achieve that goal:

Delay collections. If you are self-employed, delay year-end billings until late enough in the year that payments won't come before the end of the year.

Deferred compensation. If you are employed, negotiate a deferred compensation agreement with your employer. This type of agreement does not have retroactive effect, though. So act as soon as you can if you want the maximum deferral into next year or beyond. Many employers will agree to pay interest on the money they hold back, so you don't have to lose anything by having your compensation deferred. It is important to note that in order to achieve deferral, the arrangement must not be secured, which involves some risk depending on your employer's financial status.

Year-end bonuses. Year-end bonuses do not have to be paid before the end of the year, so strike a deal with your employer to have your bonus paid in January. Generally, your employer will not lose its deduction for the current year by delaying your payment until next year, as long as its obligation to pay you is fixed before the end of its tax year and paid within 2½ months of the close of its tax year.

Incentive stock options. If your employer gives you a qualified incentive stock option (ISO) to purchase its stock or stock in a parent or subsidiary corporation, you are not taxed until you dispose of the stock. In other words, there is no regular tax on receipt or exercise of the option, thus you may delay income by holding on to the option or stock. However, the bargain element on the option must generally be considered for AMT purposes when your rights in the option become transferable or when these rights are no longer subject to a substantial risk of forfeiture.

Interest income. Interest on Treasury bills and bank certificates having a term of one year or less is not includible in your income until you receive it at maturity. If you have funds that are now in interest-bearing accounts, you can delay tax on the interest yet to be received this year by transferring funds to these types of certificates.

Annuities. Another way to defer income is to transfer funds from interest-bearing accounts to a commercial annuity.

Maximize retirement plan contributions. Make sure that you are contributing the maximum allowable amount to your retirement plans (e.g., 401(k)s, IRAs, SEPs, and/or Keogh plans).

If you are age 50 and over, additional catch-up contributions to a traditional or Roth IRA are permitted. For 2004 and 2005, the amount of the catch-up contribution is $500. For 2006, the catch-up contribution amount increases to $1,000.

For a complete discussion of catch-up contributions, see Chapter 5, "Retirement Planning."

Like-kind exchanges. Generally, if you trade business or investment property for other business or investment property of a "like-kind", you will be able to defer recognition of gain or loss. While your gain will eventually be subject to income tax, you may be able to defer taxation for a number of years.

If you are exchanging property that you have been depreciating using MACRS, you are generally required to continue to depreciate the carryover basis of the new property (the undepreciated cost) over the remaining depreciation period as if the exchange never took place. The additional cash (if any) that you pay for the new property is recovered over the full depreciation period (27.5 years for residential rental property and 39 years for commercial property).

Example You purchased a residential rental property for $100,000 and have been depreciating it under MACRS. In the first ten years you have claimed $36,000 in depreciation. Your remaining undepreciated basis is $64,000. You now trade your property plus $50,000 for another residential rental property. Your basis in the new property is $114,000 ($50,000 cash paid plus $64,000 undepreciated basis). $50,000 of the basis will be depreciated over 27.5 years. You will continue to depreciate the $64,000 carryover basis over the remaining 17.5 years in the depreciation period as if the trade never took place. In this situation the rule is beneficial because you will be able to recover the $64,000 carryover basis in 17.5 years instead of 27.5 years.

Tax Alert Taxpayers may elect to treat the cost of certain depreciable business assets as an expense rather than a capital expenditure (Code Sec. 179). To qualify, the property must be tangible personal property that is depreciable and is acquired by purchase for use in the active conduct of a trade or business. The election, which is made on Form 4562, is attached to the taxpayer's original return (or an amended return filed by the due date of the original return, including extensions) for the year in which the property is placed in service. The maximum Code Sec. 179 deduction, as adjusted for inflation, is $105,000 for 2005. In addition to the $105,000 dollar limitation, the amount allowed must be reduced by the cost of the property to the extent the cost exceeds the investment limitation of $420,000 for 2005.

Installment sales. If you must sell property (other than stock or securities) this year, delay receipt of part of the proceeds by having the payments made to you in installments over the next few years. The installment method may allow you to reduce your total tax on the sale by preventing your taxable gain from pushing you into a higher tax bracket in the year of sale. Make sure, though, that the payments are secured and that the buyer pays interest on the unpaid balance.

Keep in mind that all depreciation recapture is reported as ordinary income in the *tax year of an installment sale*. As a result, if you are a seller you may want to negotiate an initial payment sufficient to satisfy the additional tax liability caused by the recapture. This rule, however, is not a concern if you sell real property that you depreciated using MACRS. Depreciation on MACRS real property is not subject to recapture.

Ways to Accelerate Income

A rule of thumb says you should defer income if at all possible. But in the following situations, it may pay you to accelerate your income:

- *Change in filing status.* An upcoming marriage or divorce that will put you in a higher tax bracket next year may dictate accelerating 2006 income into 2005.
- *Change in income level.* Anticipated changes in employment, sales of assets, etc., next year could put you in a higher bracket, making the tax on accelerated income lower this year.
- *Too many deductions.* If your itemized deductions exceed your taxable income this year, don't lose the excess deductions. Accelerate enough income to cover them. Follow the same strategy if you have carryover deductions from previous years that will expire this year.

Here is how you do it:

Collect receivables. If you are self-employed, make sure you do all the billing you can, and then be sure to collect! Remember, if you are using the cash method of accounting, income is not taken into account until you receive it.

Year-end bonus. If your employer pays bonuses after the end of the year or you arranged to have your bonus deferred for tax reasons, negotiate a change. Get that bonus into your hands by the end of the year.

Restricted stock. If you receive, as compensation from your employer, stock that is subject to restrictions (for example, stock that may be subject to forfeiture if your employment is terminated before a specified number of years), you generally are not taxed on the stock until it is vested. You may, however, elect to treat the stock as vested and pay the tax right away. This is done by filing a statement with the IRS within 30 days after you receive the stock. The risk in this is that you may not undo the tax damage if you later forfeit the stock. Whether you decide to make the election depends on the value of the stock at the time and on how secure you are that you will eventually be vested.

Incentive stock options. If you have an ISO that you received from your employer, exercise the option and dispose of the stock, with due regard to investment considerations.

IRA or retirement plan distributions. If you are over age 59½ and you either have a traditional IRA or are covered by an employer's retirement plan, you may increase this year's income by making withdrawals. (In the case of the retirement plan, your right to make withdrawals is determined by the plan.)

Installment notes. The installment sale you made in a previous year for the purpose of deferring taxable gain can be undone if you need the income this year rather than in the future, and there are three ways to accomplish this. The first is to arrange for your debtor (the buyer) to pay off the note before the end of the year. The second is to use the note as collateral for a loan. The third is to sell the note to a third party. In any case, the portion of the gain that you haven't yet reported will become reportable.

Dividends. If you have control over a corporation that pays you dividends, arrange for them to be paid before the end of the year.

Lawsuits, insurance claims, etc. If you have a dispute with someone you believe owes you taxable money (for example, claims for wages, damages to property in excess of the damaged property's basis, etc.), you are not taxed on the money until you are paid. One way to accelerate this income is to settle your dispute. You may take less, but you could make it up in lower taxes.

Capital gains. When dealing with capital gains, your greatest flexibility comes from your ability to decide when to sell assets. If you have assets that have appreciated in value, a sale before the end of the year can give you the income you need to meet your tax planning goals.

EE bonds. If you have elected to defer taxes on your EE bond interest, you can cash in the bonds and take the accrued interest into income.

 Tax Alert Generally, for 2005 and 2006, the maximum long-term capital gains tax rate for individuals is 15% (or 5% for individuals in the 10% or 15% income tax brackets). Higher rates apply to certain types of capital assets, such as collectibles and unrecaptured Code Sec. 1250 gain. In addition, dividend income is generally taxed at the same rate as capital gains for 2005 and 2006. Without further legislative action, dividends received by an individual after 2008 will be taxed at ordinary income tax rates. In addition, capital gains realized after 2008 will be taxed at 20% (or 10% for individuals in the 10% or 15% income tax brackets).

Taking Advantage of Flexible Spending Accounts

Setting up a flexible spending account (FSA) with your employer can result in substantial tax savings. An employee can set up an account with pre-tax wages to pay in advance for eligible health and/or dependent care expenses. There is no statutory limit on the amount of contributions that may be made to a health

FSA (although the plan must itself specify a limit in terms of a dollar amount or a percentage of compensation). However, contributions to a dependent care FSA are limited to $5,000 per year. The $5,000 limit applies whether you are single or married ($2,500 for married filing separate). Wages placed in the account are not subject to income and FICA taxes. When you incur eligible expenses, you may file a claim for reimbursement from your account. It's up to you to designate how much money you want withheld from your paycheck over the entire year and deposited to your account. Generally, the amount you specify will be prorated over the number of regular paychecks you receive in a year.

 Tax Tip Careful estimating of health care and/or dependent care expenses is crucial for using FSAs successfully. Once money is put into a spending account, it can only be used to reimburse you for qualifying current-year expenses. If your expenses during the plan year (which may include up to an additional 2½-month grace period if elected by the employer) are less than the amount in your account, any remainder will be lost.

Avoiding the Risks of Incentive Stock Options

If your employer offers you an incentive stock option, take it because this gives you the right to purchase stock of your employer, often at a discount, without recognizing income until the stock is sold.

There are, however, some risks. Although no taxable income is recognized when an option is granted or exercised, the difference between the fair market value and the exercise price is an item of AMT tax preference and can trigger a significant AMT liability in the year of exercise if a large amount of appreciated stock is involved. Generally, most of the AMT liability will be recovered in the year the stock is sold as an AMT credit against regular tax *if* the value of the stock has not decreased after the exercise of the option. This is because when you compute your alternative minimum taxable income in the year of the sale, the AMT gain is the difference between the fair market value of the stock at the time of the sale and the fair market value of the stock at the time of the exercise. Regular tax gain, however, is the difference between the fair market value at the time of the sale and the exercise price. Because your regular tax liability will exceed the AMT tentative minimum tax in this situation, most or all of the credit for the previously paid AMT is typically claimed against your regular tax in the year of sale.

 Tax Alert For high-income taxpayers, the tax rate reductions enacted under the Jobs and Growth Tax Relief Reconciliation Act of 2003 (P.L. 108-27) increased the risk of liability for AMT. To offset that risk, the 2003 Act increased the

AMT exemption amounts. For single taxpayers, the exemption amount rises to $40,250 (from $35,750), for married couples filing jointly and surviving spouses, it rises to $58,000 (from $49,000), and for married taxpayers filing separately, it rises to $29,000 (from $24,500). The increased amounts apply in 2003, 2004, and 2005.

Example In 2001, an employer gave you an incentive stock option to purchase 10,000 shares of employer stock at $10 a share. There are no tax consequences in 2001. In 2002, when the shares have a fair market value of $50, you exercise the option. The exercise has no regular income tax implications. However, for AMT purposes you have a tax preference of $400,000 (($50 - $10) x 10,000 shares). For the sake of simplicity, assume that you must pay an AMT tax liability of $112,000 on the $400,000 preference ($400,000 x 28%). Assume that your tentative minimum tax and regular tax are exactly equal in 2003, 2004, and 2005. As a result, no amount of the $112,000 AMT liability may be claimed as a credit against your regular tax in these years.

If you sell the stock in 2006 for $60 a share, you will recognize a $500,000 long-term capital gain (($60 fmv - $10 cost) x 10,000 shares) and pay a regular tax liability of $75,000 ($500,000 x 15% long-term capital gain rate) on this amount. For purposes of computing AMT liability, however, your AMT long-term capital gain is only $100,000 (($60 fmv - $50 AMT basis) x 10,000 shares) and the tentative minimum tax on the gain is only $15,000 ($100,000 x 15% long-term capital gain rate (the 15% capital gains rate applies for regular tax and AMT purposes)). Note that your AMT basis of each share of the stock is increased from $10 to $50 by the $40 gain previously recognized in 2001 for AMT purposes. Assume again for the sake of simplicity that your tentative minimum tax without regard to the AMT long-term capital gain is equal to your regular tax liability without regard to the regular tax long-term capital gain. Taking the long-term capital gain in account, your 2006 tentative minimum tax will be $60,000 less than your regular tax liability and you may claim a $60,000 AMT credit against your regular tax liability in 2006. The remaining $52,000 ($112,000 - $60,000) unused AMT credit may be claimed in future years when your regular tax liability is greater than tentative minimum tax liability.

If the price of stock drops dramatically after the exercise of an incentive stock option, it may become much more difficult to recover the previously paid AMT liability because your regular tax liability will not increase enough relative to your AMT liability to allow you to claim a significant portion of your available AMT credit.

An AMT tax preference is not created when you exercise an option if you can't sell the stock right away or it is subject to a substantial risk of forfeiture. If you receive this type of stock, however, you can make a "Code Sec. 83(b)" election for AMT purposes and take the preference into account. The election makes sense, for example, if the election will not make you subject to the AMT. By making the election, when you sell the stock, you get a higher basis for purposes of determining your AMT gain. This may keep you out of the AMT or at least reduce your AMT liability in the year of sale.

No AMT adjustment is required if you exercise an ISO and sell the stock in the same tax year. However, if you do this, you won't be able to take advantage of the long-term capital gain rates.

Planning Alert Year-end is a good time to review the holding periods of any incentive stock options (ISOs) that you have exercised. In order to obtain favorable long-term capital gain treatment, stock acquired under an ISO may not be sold before the later of two years from the date of the grant of the option, or one year from the date of exercise of the option. Thus, in addition to the usual one-year holding period for favorable long-term capital gain treatment, the special ISO holding requirements must also be met. Market forces also factor into the decision of when to exercise an ISO. The more rapidly the underlying stock appreciates, the greater the risk you will owe alternative minimum tax on the exercise of the option.

CHAPTER 3

Making Your Deductions Count

An important element of tax planning is making sure, before it's too late, that you meet the technical requirements for all of your deductions. Appendix E at the end of this book provides a checklist for deductible and nondeductible personal expenses as well as eligible business deductions.

But did you know that you may meet the technical requirements for a deduction and still lose out? The traps and the ways to avoid them are discussed below.

One significant factor to keep in mind is that many deductions may be reduced if your adjusted gross income (AGI) level is too high. For example, itemized deductions and the personal exemption ($3,200 for 2005) are phased out based on the excess of AGI over established threshold levels. Also, other deductions may be claimed only if they exceed a certain percentage of AGI (2% for miscellaneous itemized deductions, 7.5% for medical expenses, and 10% for casualty losses). Any increase to AGI operates to reduce AGI-based deductions. Accordingly, if you plan to accelerate income into 2005, be aware that not only will the additional income be taxed, but there may be fewer deductions to offset your total income amount. Appendix F at the end of this book contains a chart showing most deductions and credits that are affected by your AGI level.

2005 Phaseout Thresholds for Higher-Income Taxpayers

Filing Status	Personal Exemption Phaseout Begins:	Personal Exemption Phaseout Completed:	3% Reduction of Itemized Deductions Begins:*
Single	$145,950	$268,450	$145,950
Married, filing jointly	$218,950	$341,450	$145,950
Head-of-household	$182,450	$304,950	$145,950
Married, filing separately	$109,475	$170,725	$72,975
			*Reduction is limited to 80% of your deductions

 **Tax Alert** Beginning in 2006, the limit on itemized deductions for high income taxpayers will be phased out until it is fully repealed in 2010.

Maximizing the Value of Itemized Deductions

Every year you are forced either to pass up legitimate itemized deductions or to lose the standard deduction. It's built into the system; you get one or the other. And the loss can be considerable. For 2005, the standard deduction is as follows, depending on your filing status:

2005 Standard Deductions

If your Filing Status is:	Your Standard Deduction is:
Single	$5,000
Married filing joint return or Qualifying widow(er) with dependent child	$10,000
Married filing separate return	$5,000
Head of Household	$7,300

 Tax Alert The basic standard deduction is increased for married couples who file jointly to twice the amount of a single person in 2005. If you are married and file joint returns with your spouse, you should make a calculation to determine whether you would be better off claiming the increased standard deduction instead of itemizing your deductions. However, as a result of the change, electing married filing separately status will be no benefit to married couples since the standard deduction and tax-rate table breakpoints for couples who file jointly are simply split between the two spouses.

If you are blind or age 65 or older, you are entitled to the regular standard deduction plus $1,000 if you are married ($2,000 if you are age 65 or older and blind) or $1,250 if you are single or head of household ($2,500 if you are age 65 or older and blind).

**2005 Standard Deduction Chart for
People Age 65 or Older or Blind**

Check the correct number of boxes below.

Then go to the chart.

You   65 or older _____ Blind _____

Your spouse, if claiming spouse's exemption 65 or older _____ Blind _____

Total number of boxes you checked _____

If Your Filing Status is:	And the # in the Box Above is:	Your Standard Deduction is:
Single	1	$6,250
	2	7,500
Married filing joint return or Qualifying widow(er) with dependent child	1	11,000
	2	12,000
	3	13,000
	4	14,000
Married filing separate return	1	6,000
	2	7,000
	3	8,000
	4	9,000
Head of Household	1	8,550
	2	9,800

If you itemize, you lose the standard deduction. On the other hand, if your itemized deductions are insufficient and you take the standard deduction, the itemized deductions you do have are out the window. But it doesn't have to be that way! You can have your cake and eat it too with careful planning and a technique known as "bunching."

Here is how bunching works:

 Example You are single. Your expenses are pretty constant from year to year, with the itemizable
expenses running as follows:

Mortgage interest	$ 1,700
Medical (deductible portion)	900
State and local taxes	950
Charitable contributions	2,050
Total	$ 5,600

That's enough to itemize, but you lose the standard deduction, which is $5,000 for 2005. Over two years, you will be entitled to deduct $11,200, but that's it.

Bunching allows you to adjust the timing of your expenses so they are high in one year and low in the next. Following this strategy, you may be able to make the following adjustments:

- In even years, prepay January interest in December.
- See the dentist in January, June and December in even years and June in odd years. Nonemergency medical treatment can be adjusted in a similar way.
- In even years, prepay property taxes due in the following year.
- Plan large charitable gifts for even years.

Following this strategy, you end up with the following expenses for 2005 and 2006:

	2005	2006
Mortgage interest	$1,842	$1,558
Medical (deductible portion)	1,500	300
State and local taxes	1,300	600
Charitable contributions	3,450	650
Total	$8,092	$3,108

The total of itemized deductions is the same, $11,200 for two years. However, by bunching your expenses, you get $8,092 of itemized deductions in 2005 and a standard deduction of approximately $5,100 for 2006 (the 2006 figure was not yet available from the IRS at the time of publication). Total: $13,192. You've still lost the standard deduction in 2005, but you've reduced your lost itemized deductions by moving them from 2006 to 2005. That's a $1,992 improvement, saving you $498 if you are in the 25% bracket ($1,992 x 25% = $498). You may be able to do even better.

The strategy of bunching itemized deductions is most effective if your average deductions approximately equal your standard deduction. The strategy will not work unless you can reduce your itemized deductions below your standard deduction amount in the nonbunching year.

If your 2005 adjusted gross income (AGI) exceeds $145,950 ($72,975 if you are married and file separately), bunching may not help. If you fall into this category, you may be subject to a rule that reduces your itemized deductions on a sliding scale that could eliminate as much as 80% of them. If you find that you are subject to this phaseout of your itemized deductions, your aim should be to shift your itemized deductions to years in which your income is lower.

 Legislation Highlight Under the American Jobs Creation Act of 2004 (P.L. 108-357), taxpayers may elect to deduct state and local sales tax in lieu of state and local income tax. If taxpayers elect to deduct sales taxes, they may either claim the total amount paid, which requires substantiation with receipts, or they may deduct an amount taken from IRS tables, in addition to amounts actually paid as sales tax for certain items (such as a motor vehicle or a boat). The deduction for state and local sales tax is subject to phaseout limitations and is a preference item for AMT purposes.

Based on IRS statistics, CCH editors have prepared a chart that shows the average amounts of itemized deductions claimed on 2003 returns for medical expenses, taxes, interest and charitable contributions. See Appendix D.

Caution: The chart is for general informational purposes only. Taxpayers who claim deductions on their federal income tax returns cannot rely on averages; they must be prepared to substantiate their deductions with the required documentation.

Avoiding the 2% Trap of Miscellaneous Itemized Deductions

Did you know that you can lose hundreds or even thousands of dollars in deductions for expenses which fall in the category of miscellaneous itemized deductions? Such expenses are deductible only to the extent that they total more than 2% of adjusted gross income (AGI). If your AGI is $60,000, that means that you could lose as much as $1,200 in deductions each year.

Which deductions are affected? Miscellaneous itemized deductions include expenses to produce or collect income; to manage, conserve or maintain property held for producing income; or to determine, contest, pay, or claim a refund of any tax. Other miscellaneous itemized deductions are unreimbursed expenses you incur as an employee (e.g., travel, meals, lodging, education, equipment, special clothing, or professional dues).

 Tax Alert The Military Family Tax Relief Act of 2003 (P.L. 108-121) created an above-the-line deduction available for travel expenses of all National Guard troops and Reservists, regardless of whether they itemize deductions. Travel must take the National Guard soldier or Reservist more than 100 miles away from their home and require an overnight stay. The deduction applies to amounts paid or incurred beginning in 2003.

You will be able to avoid the "2% trap" if you are a "statutory employee." Employees that come within this category are able to claim their unreimbursed business expenses as a direct deduction from gross income and thus they are able to ignore the restrictions placed on miscellaneous itemized deductions. Box 13 of your Form W-2 should indicate if you are classified as a statutory employee. The classification includes full-time life insurance salespersons, certain agent or commission drivers, a limited group of traveling salespersons, and certain home workers.

Tax Tip As year-end approaches, you should make sure that you have substantiated all of your business expenses to your employer or have returned any amounts paid under an accountable plan in excess of substantiated expenses. As a general rule, expenses should be substantiated within 60 days after they are incurred. Excess reimbursements should be repaid to the employer within 120 days after the employer makes the reimbursement, or within 120 days after the statement date (if periodic or quarterly statements are used to show the employee where he stands).

Tax Tip Bunching pays off for your unreimbursed employee business expenses, as it does with regular itemized deductions. Shift your expenses as much as possible to fall in alternate years. Pick the year in which you expect the lower AGI to pay the majority of the expenses. That's when the deduction floor will be the lowest. Let your "good year" be the low-expense year. You're going to lose the deductions anyway, so the level of the deduction floor doesn't matter.

Minimizing the Effect of 7.5% AGI Floor on Medical Expenses

Within certain limits, you may deduct expenses incurred for medical care for yourself, your spouse and your dependents. Medical care includes amounts paid for:

(1)   the diagnosis, mitigation, treatment, or prevention of disease or for the purpose of affecting any structure or function of the body,

(2)   transportation primarily for and essential to medical care,

(3)   insurance covering medical care,

(4)   lodging while away from home primarily for and essential to medical care,

(5)   accommodating a home to the needs of a physically handicapped individual,

(6)   prescription drugs and insulin, and

(7)   qualified long-term care services and certain long-term care insurance premiums.

The IRS has recently ruled that expenses for certain weight-loss programs may be deducted as a medical expense. The program must be undertaken as treatment for a specific disease or diseases (including obesity) diagnosed by a physician.

Medical expenses may be deducted only to the extent that they exceed 7.5% of your adjusted gross income.

Tax Tip Whenever there is a deduction floor for expenses there is an opportunity for bunching. Medical expenses are no exception. If you have elective medical, dental or counseling expenses, do a little shifting to have them fall, as much as possible, in alternate years. For example, if you are nearing the 7.5% floor or have surpassed it for this year, you may consider scheduling additional medical treatment before the end of the year. Conversely, if you have not reached the threshold and know that an expensive operation must be had next year, try to delay any further treatment until next year. Remember, although expenses that are reimbursed by insurance are not deductible, health insurance premiums are.

Additional Medical Expense Planning

You and other members of your family may be paying substantial amounts for the care of elderly parents who are in a nursing home. Some or all of these payments may qualify as medical expenses if you claim the parent as a dependent on your return. You can maximize potential tax savings by paying all or most of the expenses in one year yourself and then have others take their turns and reap the benefit of the dependency deduction and medical expense deduction in later years. In other words, rotate payment of the medical expenses on an annual basis.

Some or all of the premiums paid for long-term care insurance are deductible as a medical expense (subject to the 7.5% AGI floor). Benefits paid under the policy are not usually taxable. The following chart shows the 2005 deduction limits that are based on age.

2005 Deductible Long-Term Care Premiums

Age of Beneficiary	Maximum Deduction
40 or less	$270
41-50	$510
51-60	$1,020
61-70	$2,720
Over 70	$3,400

The cost of home improvements that are necessary because of your medical condition may qualify as a medical expense but only to the extent that the improvements do not increase the value of your home.

If you or your spouse have large medical expenses you may be able to save taxes by filing separate returns. This is because the 7.5% AGI floor is computed separately for each of you based on your own income. Compute your taxes using joint returns and separate returns to see if this will work for you.

Your employer may offer medical flexible savings arrangements which allow you to contribute pre-tax earnings up to the limit specified in the plan. You will forfeit any amount that you do not use to pay medical expenses by the end of the year. The year-end purchase of eyeglasses and contact lenses is one way to ensure that you will not forfeit any unspent contributions. See page 22.

 Planning Alert The 10% penalty on early distributions from IRA plans does not apply if the distribution is used to pay unreimbursed medical expenses that exceed 7.5% of AGI. In addition, if certain requirements are met, the 10% penalty will not apply to IRA distributions that are used to pay for health insurance premiums for unemployed individuals. The rules for avoiding the 10% penalty are complex and you should consult your tax advisor before taking any action.

 Planning Alert The Medicare Prescription Drug, Improvement, and Modernization Act of 2003 (P.L. 108-173) created Health Savings Accounts (HSAs), a pre-tax savings option to help workers cope with rising health care costs. HSAs enable workers with high deductible health insurance to make pre-tax contributions of up to an annual limit (the 2005 limit is $2,650, or $5,250 for families) each year to cover health care costs. Any amount paid or distributed from an HSA which is used exclusively to pay the qualified medical expenses of an account beneficiary is not included in gross income.

Multi-Year Planning for AMT

If you tend to be a borderline candidate for the alternative minimum tax (AMT) (that is, your AMT tentative tax and regular tax are approximately equal from year to year), your best bet is to keep it that way. Do not start bunching your itemized deductions because you will end up losing their value in the regular tax year.

If your deductions are not so evenly spaced and you have AMT years and non-AMT years, the name of the game is brinkmanship. Shift your preferences from the AMT year to the non-AMT year until you get to the brink of AMT liability, reducing your regular tax to the point where it equals the tentative tax. This technique gives you maximum use of your preference deductions.

Many high-income individuals may be trapped by the AMT even if they don't engage heavily in the kind of investment and business activity that generates AMT preferences and adjustments. The reason is that Schedule A deductions for state and local income taxes, real property taxes or general state and local sales taxes, miscellaneous itemized deductions, and personal exemptions all are disallowed for AMT purposes. These deductions must be added back to taxable income to arrive at AMTI. In addition, interest paid on home-equity debt may not be deductible for AMT purposes even though such interest paid on up to $100,000 of debt can be claimed to arrive at the regular tax.

Timing strategies are also effective for nonpreference adjustments. If you are subject to the AMT in one year and not in the next, figure out your marginal rate in the regular tax year. If the rate is more than 26% or 28%, shift nonpreference deductions to the regular tax year. If your regular tax rate will be 15%, go the other way: shift the nonpreference deductions into the AMT year.

Working with the interaction between the AMT and the regular tax can be a logistical nightmare, but careful planning can pay off.

Qualifying for Deductions

Clinching your deductions is a critical phase of your year-end tax work. When you sit down early next year to work on your 2005 taxes, don't let yourself be surprised to find that you didn't quite qualify for a deduction you thought you had. Avoid that problem by reviewing your situation now when it's not too late to pick up the loose ends.

Here are the important points to remember if you are a cash-method taxpayer:

Deduct in the year you pay. Accrual-method taxpayers generally deduct when they place an order, sign a contract, or otherwise incur the obligation to pay and economic performance has occurred. But most individuals are not on the accrual method. For a cash-method taxpayer, the key date is when a deductible expense is actually paid.

Payment by check. Date your checks before year-end and put them in the mail before January 1, 2006. This meets the payment requirement for cash-method taxpayers and it gives you a record, in case you are ever called on to prove the deduction.

No IOUs. Giving a seller or service provider a note or other promise to pay does not qualify you to deduct the expense until you pay it off. If you have any outstanding IOUs and you want to deduct the expense this year, pay them off now.

Credit cards are okay. A good alternative to paying an expense by check is to pay by credit card (Visa, Master Card, Discover, or American Express can be used to pay your taxes). The rule against IOUs doesn't apply here because a third party, the credit card company is involved. However, you will also pay substantial interest to the credit card company for each month that the credit card loan is outstanding.

Finance your expenses with a bank loan. Take out a bank loan to pay deductible expenses before the end of the year. If the loan is used to pay business expenses, you may deduct the interest, unless the loan pertains to business expenses incurred as an employee. If it is used to pay itemizable or other personal expenses, think about a home equity loan. Otherwise the interest won't be deductible.

Beyond that, it's important to consider what must be done to complete your entitlement on a deduction-by-deduction basis. What follows is a run down of some common deductions that can be most affected by your year-end actions.

Maximize Your Charitable Contribution Deduction

Charitable contributions are possibly the most flexible of deductible expenses from a planning standpoint because their timing is usually completely discretionary. Your year-end evaluation of the need for deductions in this year or the next should determine whether you make a gift in December or January.

If you decide that you need the deduction this year, a mere pledge is not enough. You have to pay the pledge before the end of the year. On the other hand, if you decide you need the deduction next year, feel free to pledge now. The pledge could help the charity get financing or matching funds now, but you won't have the deduction until you pay the pledge after the first of the year.

Gifts of property require special attention at this time of year. As a general rule, gifts of appreciated property (such as stock) have a very significant tax advantage: you get a charitable contribution deduction for the full appreciated value of the property, both for regular tax purposes and AMT purposes, and you avoid paying tax on the capital gain you would have if you sold the property and then contributed the proceeds.

Charitable contributions of $250 or more generally must be substantiated to be deductible. As substantiation, you must receive a contemporaneous written acknowledgment from the recipient organization. The substantiation must include a good-faith estimate of the value of any goods or services provided to you in exchange for the contribution. The burden is placed on individuals who itemize their deductions to request written substantiation because they may no longer rely solely on a canceled check to back up their deduction.

In addition to outright gifts of cash or property, there are a number of other ways in which contributions may be made to a charity.

Deferred gift annuities. You may donate cash or property to a charity in return for an annuity that begins when you retire. You get a deduction now for the difference between the value of the annuity and the value of the property contributed. The amount of the deduction depends on how long you wait to receive your annuity. It gets larger the longer you wait. A portion of each annuity payment is excluded from income until the original investment in the contract is recovered. This is the same rule that applies to commercial annuities.

Charitable remainder trusts. You may set up a trust and transfer appreciated property, such as land or stock. You retain a life interest in the income from the property and give the remainder to the designated charity. You don't pay any tax as the result of the transfer of the property or the sale of the property by the trust. You get a charitable contribution for the value of the remainder interest when you set up the trust.

Generally, your income from the trust may be determined in one of two ways. You can choose to receive a fixed annual percentage of the fair market value of the trust property. Fair market value is measured at the time the trust is set up. If the income from the trust property is not sufficient to pay the annuity, the trust will use the trust property (e.g., sell it) to pay you. Alternatively, you can choose to receive an annuity that is based upon a percentage of the value of the trust property determined annually. Thus, if the value of the trust property appreciates, your annuity for that year increases.

Pooled income fund. You may contribute property along with others to a particular charity's fund (contributions are "pooled"). In return you obtain a share of the income based upon the annual performance of the pooled fund. You obtain an immediate charitable contribution deduction based upon the difference between your retained interest and the fair market value of the contributed property. One advantage of contributing to a pooled fund is that you avoid the cost of setting up your own charitable remainder trust.

Try to Collect on Debts

If you have loaned someone money and are now unable to collect the amount owed to you, you may be able to claim a deduction for a bad debt. There is a distinction between nonbusiness bad debts and business bad debts, and the rules are different for each.

You may deduct a nonbusiness bad debt only in the year in which the debt becomes totally worthless. You may deduct a partially worthless business debt when the uncollectible amount can be identified with reasonable certainty.

 Tax Tip If you have a worthless debt owed to you, it is important that you begin efforts to collect the debt well before the end of the year. These efforts should provide you with the evidence you need to prove the debt's worthlessness or you'll collect the debt. Either way, you're money ahead.

Protect Your Business Expense Deductions

Do you free-lance, have a business on the side, or have a hobby that provides you with income? If you do, year-end is the time to take steps to protect the deductions you might be entitled to for your expenses.

The problem is that most expenses are deductible only if you are in a "trade or business." If the IRS successfully characterizes your activity as a hobby, the deductions are generally available only up to the amount of your income from the activity. It is often difficult to distinguish between a hobby and a business, so the rules presume that you are in a business if you have a profit in any three of five consecutive years ending with the year in question (two out of seven years if you are involved in the breeding, training, showing, or racing of horses).

 Tax Tip If you have had at least three profitable years during the last four, you don't have to worry. You will be entitled to a full deduction for your expenses this year even if this is a loss year. If you haven't yet met this requirement, you should take steps now to increase your income from the activity and/or decrease your expenses. Otherwise, your deductions could be lost. Furthermore, if you can arrange for this year to be your third profitable year out of four, you will protect your deductions for next year.

Accelerate Depreciation on Your Business Assets

Depreciable business and investment assets purchased after 1986 are depreciated using the Modified Accelerated Cost Recovery System (MACRS). Under MACRS, the cost of residential rental property is recovered over 27.5 years at an even rate using the straight-line method. Commercial property is also depreciated using the straight-line method but over a 39-year recovery period.

If you are purchasing or constructing residential rental or commercial property, you may be able to recover the cost of some parts of the property over a shorter recovery period. For example, the cost attributable to a parking lot is a land improvement and may be depreciated over 15 years. Elements within the building itself, such as wiring for special machinery and removable wall coverings or carpeting, may also be depreciated separately as personal property. Neon signs and ornamental features unrelated to the operation of the building may be separately depreciated. However, you will need to document the costs of such items carefully. Your tax advisor may suggest that you hire a firm that specializes in "cost segregation" studies to determine all eligible property that can be separately depreciated. Such a study can easily pay for itself in tax savings.

 Legislation Highlight The American Jobs Creation Act of 2004 (P.L. 108-357) made several changes with respect to depreciation of business assets. See page 122 regarding limitations on expensing and depreciation of vehicles, including sports utility vehicles (SUVs). One change made by the Jobs Act is the creation of a 15-year recovery period for "qualified leasehold improvement property." The new law requires the use of straight-line depreciation for such property (in contrast to the 150 percent declining balance method usually applicable to 15-year MACRS property). This provision is not elective; if the qualifications are met, then the property must be depreciated over 15 years using the straight-line method. Qualified leasehold improvement property is any improvement to an interior portion of nonresidential real property if certain requirements are satisfied. The law applies to property placed in service after October 22, 2004 and prior to January 1, 2006.

Depreciation recapture does not apply to MACRS real property but does apply to personal property (i.e., property that is not real property). When depreciation recapture applies and you sell the property, any depreciation that you claimed is taxed as ordinary income to the extent of your taxable gain. The excess gain, if any, is eligible for capital gain treatment.

The depreciation period and method for personal property under MACRS depends upon the type of asset or the business activity that you are engaged in. Generally, you should use the period and method that result in the quickest recovery of the cost of the asset. However, if you are in a low tax bracket and anticipate moving to a higher bracket later on, it may be advantageous to elect a MACRS method and recovery period that delays your deductions, such as the MACRS alternative depreciation system (ADS).

Personal property is usually depreciated using the half-year convention under MACRS. The half-year convention allows you to claim one-half of a full year's depreciation in the year you purchase an asset (i.e., "place it in service"). However, you are subject to the mid-quarter convention if the total cost of personal property that you place in service during the last three months of the year exceeds 40 percent of the total cost of all personal property placed in service during the year.

Generally, the mid-quarter convention results in less overall depreciation than the half-year convention. However, if you are able to time the purchase of your assets you may be able to get an increased depreciation deduction using the mid-quarter convention in the first-year of the depreciation period. The mid-quarter convention produces the best potential for tax savings when assets with the shortest recovery periods and highest costs are placed in service during the first quarter.

 Example You place 3-year MACRS property costing $550 in service in the first quarter. 10-year MACRS property costing $450 is placed in service in the last quarter of the year. The mid-quarter convention applies because more than 40% of the total cost ($1,000) is in the last quarter. Under the mid-quarter convention, you claim $321 ($550 x 58.33%) on the 3-year property and $11 ($450 x 2.5%) on the 10-year property for a total deduction of $332. If the half-year convention applies, your depreciation deduction on the 3-year property is $183 ($550 x 33.33%) and $45 ($450 x 10%) on the 10-year property for a total of $228.

Expensing Business Assets Under Code Sec. 179

If you own your own business, you are also allowed to "write-off" as an expense up to an annual dollar amount a portion of the cost of depreciable personal property that you place in service during the year rather than treating the cost as a capital expenditure. This expense deduction is referred to as a "Section 179" deduction.

 Tax Alert For 2003, the annual dollar limitation was increased from $25,000 to $100,000 and the annual investment limitation from $200,000 to $400,000. For 2004 and 2005, the annual dollar limitation and the annual investment limitation have been adjusted for inflation; for 2005, the annual dollar limitation is $105,000, and the annual investment limitation is $420,000. Qualifying property is defined as depreciable tangible personal property that is purchased for use in the active conduct of a trade or business. The American Jobs Creation Act of 2004 (P.L. 108-357) extended the higher limitation amounts through 2007, including annual adjustment of those amounts for inflation. Without future Congressional action, in 2008, the annual dollar limitation will return to $25,000 and the annual investment limitation will return to $100,000.

If the value of the qualifying property that you place in service during a tax year exceeds the investment limitation ($420,000 for 2005) plus the applicable dollar limit for the year ($105,000 in 2005), you may not claim the expense deduction. The amount that you expense is also limited to the amount of your taxable income from all of your trades and businesses. Wage and salary income is treated as taxable income from a trade or business for this purpose. Thus, if you have at least $105,000 of wage income in 2005, you can claim the full expense deduction even if your business is operating at a loss.

Any amounts expensed under Code Sec. 179 are not taken into account in determining whether the mid-quarter convention applies to assets that are not expensed. Thus, by expensing assets placed in service in the first three quarters you may be able to qualify for the mid-quarter convention.

Conversely, you may be able to avoid the mid-quarter convention by expensing assets placed in service in the last quarter.

Generally, you will want to expense as much as the law allows. If you place more than $105,000 of assets in service during the year, you should expense the assets with the longest MACRS recovery period. For example, given the choice, it's better to expense 10-year property than 3-year property. If you expense the 3-year property first, it will take you 10 years to recover the remaining cost of the 10-year property. If you expense the 10-year property first, it will only take three years to recover the remaining cost of the 3-year property.

The Section 179 expense deduction is not an item of alternative minimum tax preference or adjustment. Therefore, if you are subject to the AMT, you may want to consider expensing depreciable property that could generate an AMT depreciation adjustment.

 Planning Alert Usually, you should not expense any portion of an automobile. This is because annual depreciation caps limit depreciation deductions on an automobile and the Sec. 179 expense allowance is treated as a depreciation deduction for this purpose. If the mid-quarter convention applies to the vehicle, however, the regular first-year depreciation deduction may be less than the applicable first-year cap if the car was purchased in the last half of the year. If so, you may want to expense the difference between the first-year cap and the depreciation deduction.

Seller-Paid Points—A Deduction for Home Buyers

If you purchased a home and the seller paid the mortgage points, then the seller is treated as having paid the amount of such points to you. You, in turn, are treated as having used this cash to pay the points charged by the lender and you may deduct them. For tax purposes, the cost of the home is reduced by the amount of the seller's payment in computing your basis.

Benefits of Renting Your Vacation Home

A vacation or main home, a source of pleasure for you and your family, can also be a source of tax benefits if you rent it out. The degree of benefit depends on how much time you spend there and how much time you rent it out.

If you rent out your vacation or main home for less than 15 days during the year, the rental income is tax free. But you will only be able to deduct real estate taxes, mortgage interest, and casualty losses. Deductions for maintenance and repairs are not allowed.

On the other hand, if you rent out the home for 15 days or more during the year, you must include the rent in income and you may deduct all of these expenses, provided your personal use does not exceed the larger of 14 days or 10% of the rental days. A fix-up day does not count as a personal use day even if the rest of the family comes along for a day of recreation. If you exceed these limits, your deductions are scaled down.

Investment Decisions

If you have a gain from your investment transaction, it will be taxed as either ordinary income or as a capital gain, depending on the circumstances. If you have a capital gain, you will have to identify it as either long-term or short-term. A capital gain is long-term if the asset sold was held for more than 12 months. The correct classification and identification will help you figure the tax treatment on your investment gain.

As an economic incentive to save and invest, gain from the sale of a capital asset is normally taxed at a rate that is lower than ordinary income tax rates if the requirements, such as the holding period, are met. As a general rule, for 2005, the maximum long-term capital gains tax rate for individuals is 15% (5% if you are in a 10% or 15% tax bracket). These rates apply for both regular tax and alternative minimum tax purposes. If you are like most people and recognize capital gains mostly from the sale or exchange of capital assets such as stocks, bonds, and mutual funds, this is your top tax rate for these gains.

Tax Tip The 15% and 5% long-term capital gains rates do not apply to all types of capital assets. A maximum 28% rate is imposed on long-term gain from collectibles and net gain from small business stock. There is also a maximum rate of 25% imposed on unrecaptured Section 1250 gain. Some members of Congress have indicated that they want to lower the maximum 28% capital gains tax rate on some types of collectibles.

Tax Alert Remember that short-term capital gains are taxed at your highest marginal tax rate and not the special long-term rates. It is to your advantage to make sure you hold a capital asset for "more than one year" if you have a gain and you want to achieve maximum tax savings.

Example Example 1: Mary Croft is in a 35% marginal tax rate for 2005. She sold stock that she owned for 11 months and recognized a short-term capital gain of $1,000. Her income tax on the $1,000 gain is $350 ($1,000 x 35%).

 Example Example 2: Assume the same facts as in Example 1 except that Mary owned the stock more than one year. In this event, her long-term capital gains tax on the $1,000 recognized gain would be $150 ($1,000 x 15%). Thus, she has able to achieve tax savings of $200 by owning the stock more than one year.

 Planning Alert Under current law, the capital gains rate that applies to individuals in the 10% or 15% tax bracket will fall to zero in 2008. Without further legislative action, the maximum capital gains rates after 2008 will be 20% for individuals in the 25% or higher tax brackets, and 10% for individuals in the 10% and 15% tax brackets.

Determining Holding Period

When determining how long an asset is held, the holding period begins on the day after the day the property was acquired. The same date of each following month is the beginning of a new month regardless of the number of days in the preceding month. For example, if property was acquired on February 2, 2005, the holding period began on February 3, 2005. On March 3, 2005, the individual would have held the property for one month. The date the asset is disposed of is part of the holding period. Generally, for publicly traded securities, the holding period begins the day after the "trade date" on which the securities were purchased and ends on the "trade date" of the sale. "Settlement dates" are ignored in determining the holding period.

 Tax Tip The difference between the highest tax bracket rate and the capital gains rate is 20 percentage points (35% less 15%). This makes planning to realize long-term capital gain instead of either short-term gain or ordinary income very valuable to those individuals in the higher brackets. Of course, all individuals, even those in the lowest tax bracket (i.e., 10%) will still realize a tax savings by having long-term capital gains taxed at rates lower than the generally applied income tax rates.

Capital Losses

If your capital losses are more than your capital gains, you can claim a capital loss deduction. However, your allowable capital loss deduction for the current tax year is the lesser of:

(1) $3,000 ($1,500 if you are married and file a separate return); or

(2)   your total net capital loss as shown on your Schedule D.

You can use your total net loss to reduce your income dollar for dollar. However, for the current tax year, you may not use more than $3,000 in net capital losses as an offset against other types of income.

 Example During 2005, Sam Young sold shares of stock and realized a capital loss of $5,000. Sam has no other capital transactions during the year. For 2005, Sam's only income was $45,000 in wages and $500 in taxable interest income. In determining his income tax for 2005, he may use $3,000 of his $5,000 capital loss as a deduction against his other income.

If you have a total net capital loss that is more than the yearly limit on capital loss deductions (i.e., $3,000), you can carry over the unused part to the next year and treat it as if you had incurred it in that year. If part of the loss is still unused, you can carry it over to later tax years until it is completely used up.

 Tax Tip When you carry over a loss, it retains its character of "long-term" or "short-term." Under this rule, a long-term capital loss you carry over to the next tax year will reduce that year's long-term capital gains before it reduces that year's short-term capital gains.

Determining the amount of your capital loss carryover can be a bit more complicated than you might think. The following rule applies in computing the amount of your carryover: The amount of your capital loss carryover is the amount of your total net loss that is more than the lesser of:

(1)   your allowable capital loss deduction for the year; or

(2)   your taxable income increased by your allowable capital loss deduction for the year and your deduction for personal exemptions.

Worthless Securities

If you own stock or bonds that become worthless, your loss is recognized as if you sold the security on the last day of the tax year in which it became worthless. This rule affects whether your capital loss is long-term or short-term.

Example Donna Miller purchased 100 shares of Zioam, Inc. on December 10, 2004, for a total price of $1,000. On March 3, 2005, she was notified that the shares were worthless. Donna must treat the shares as though they became worthless on December 31, 2005. As a result, even though she only owned the shares for less than three months, Donna reports a long-term capital loss on her 2005 tax return.

 Tax Alert In order to claim a loss for worthless securities you must be able to show that the securities are totally worthless. A deduction for partial worthlessness is not allowed. To prove worthless you should secure a statement from a third-party (e.g., your broker or bankruptcy court), or the company that issued the security, stating that the security is worthless.

Planning Your Investment Transactions

In order to achieve the desired goal of paying the least amount of income tax on your capital gains, you must determine which capital gains and losses you will take before the end of 2005. To effectively plan your investment transactions for the year, you must have at least a fundamental understanding of how the tax law requires you to net or "offset" your various types of capital gains and losses. Only by following the proper netting strategies can you pay the least amount of income tax.

One of the basic netting procedures provides that your short-term capital losses (i.e., losses from property held 12 months or less) are applied first against short-term gains. At this point, if you have a net short-term loss, it would be applied against your net long-term capital gain. If you had a net-short term gain after netting against long-term losses, your short-term gain will be taxed at your ordinary income tax rate, which can be as high as 35% in 2005. However, the netting process also allows you to offset your net long-term capital loss against any net short-term capital gain. The following examples illustrate how proper timing on the recognition of a long-term capital loss allows you to reduce the tax that would otherwise be payable on a net short-term gain.

 Example On November 2, 2004, John Aubrey purchased 100 shares of Gizmo Inc. for $5,000. On May 8, 2005, he sold the 100 shares for $20,000 and realized a taxable short-term capital gain of $15,000. Assume that Aubrey is in the 35% tax bracket for 2005. If he has no other capital losses to offset all or part of his short-term capital gain, he will pay $5,250 in federal income tax on the gain ($15,000 x 35%). Because it is short-term, his capital gain will be taxed as ordinary income (i.e., at the same rate as interest or wage income).

Example Assume the same facts as above, except that on December 31, 2005, Aubrey sells empty land that he has purchased a number of years ago as an investment. His cost basis in the land at the time of sale is $20,000. Because of a depressed real estate market in the area where the land is located, he only receives $12,000 for the land. Aubrey can use his $8,000 long-term loss from the sale of the land as an offset to his $15,000 short-term gain. As a result, his recognized short-term gain for 2005 is $7,000 ($15,000 gain - $8,000 loss). The tax on the gain will be $2,450 ($7,000 x 35%). Because of his sale of the land in 2005, he reduced his 2005 tax liability by $2,800 ($5,250 potential capital gains tax - $2,450 actual capital gains tax).

Planning Alert The potential impact of income tax plays an important role in your investment decisions. However, tax considerations alone should not dictate whether you buy or sell a capital asset. Your ultimate decision should be based upon the asset's potential for growth and how it compares to the growth potential for other capital assets.

Dividend Income

Prior to 2003, dividends that you received on stock were taxed as ordinary income. In other words, if you received $1,000 in dividends and you were in the 35% tax bracket, you paid $350 in tax on your dividend income. However, after 2002, "qualified dividends" paid by domestic corporations (and by qualified foreign corporations) are taxed at the same rates as long-term capital gains. If you are in the 25% or higher tax bracket, your tax on your dividend income is computed using a 15% rate. If you are in the 10% or 15% tax brackets, your tax on your dividend income is computed using a 5% rate.

Planning Alert Under current law, the rate of tax on qualified dividends received by individuals in the 10% or 15% tax bracket will fall to zero in 2008. However, without further legislative action, dividends (whether qualified or not) received after 2008 will no longer be taxed at the same rates as long-term capital gains. Instead, dividends received by all individuals (regardless of your tax bracket) will generally be taxed as ordinary income.

Certain types of dividend income are specifically excluded from the definition of "qualified dividend" for purposes of the lower rates. Dividends that are ineligible for the reduced rates include:

(1) dividends paid by credit unions, mutual insurance companies, organizations exempt from tax under Code Sec. 501, and ESOPs;

(2) if you did not hold the common stock for at least 61 days during the 121-day period beginning 60 days before the ex-dividend date; and

(3) if the receipt of the dividend causes you to be obligated to make payments on property that is substantially similar to the stock or property that is related to the stock.

Planning Alert For purposes of the holding period, the "ex-dividend date" is the first date that the buyer will not be entitled to receive that dividend. A person who buys stock the day before the ex-dividend date will receive a dividend, while a person who buys the stock on the ex-dividend date will not.

Example Mary Croft purchased 5,000 shares of Tybar Corp. common stock on July 1, 2005. The corporation paid a cash dividend of 10 cents per share. The ex-dividend date was July 8, 2005. Mary received $500 in dividends a few weeks later, and on August 4, 2005, she sold the 5,000 shares. She held the shares for 34 days (i.e., from July 2, 2005, through August 4, 2005). The 121-day period began on May 9, 2005 (60 days before the ex-dividend date), and ended on September 6, 2005 (60 days after the ex-dividend date). Under these facts, the $500 in dividends that Mary received were not "qualified dividends" because she did not hold the shares for at least 61 days during the 121-day time period. As a result, the dividends were not eligible to be taxed under the 15% maximum rate that applies to qualified dividends.

Example Assume the same facts as above, except that Mary purchased the shares on July 7, 2005 (the day before the ex-dividend date), and she sold the stock on September 8, 2005. She held the stock for 63 days (i.e., from July 8, 2005, through September 8, 2005). The $500 in dividends that she received would be treated as "qualified dividends" because she held the stock for at least 61 days of the 121-day period. As a result, the dividends would be taxed at the maximum capital gains rate of 15% (or the maximum rate of 5% if Mary is in a 10% or 15% tax bracket).

Planning Alert In the case of preferred stock, you must have held the stock more than 90 days during the 181-day period that begins 90 days before the ex-dividend date if the dividends are attributable to periods totaling more than 366 days. If the preferred dividends are attributable to periods totaling less than 367 days, the holding period mentioned above for common stock applies.

Shifting Capital Gains Tax Through Gifts

If you are in a 25% tax bracket or higher, you have an incentive to give stock or mutual funds to children or grandchildren who are in a 10% or 15% tax bracket. By making the gift, you will not only be lowering your income tax but you will probably ensure that any gain is taxed at the lowest capital gains tax rate of 5% (zero-percent in 2008). Substantial tax savings can be achieved by these gifts.

Example Judy Smith has owned 100 shares of Yawl Inc. for two years. Her basis in the stock is $1,000 and its current fair market value is $6,000. Assume Judy is in the 35% tax bracket. Her son Bill is getting married in October 2005 and Judy sells the stock in order to give him a wedding gift of $6,000 in cash. If she sells the stock at its current fair market value, her maximum capital gains tax on her $5,000 gain would be $750 ($5,000 x 15%).

Example Assume the same facts as above, except that Judy gives the shares to her son, Bill, as a wedding gift on October 1, 2005. Bill, who is in the 15% tax bracket, sells the stock on November 1, 2005, for $6,000. Because the stock was a gift to him, and its fair market value was equal to or greater than his mother's basis in the stock at the time of the gift, his basis in the stock is the same as his mother's (i.e., $1,000). Thus, he would be required to recognize a $5,000 capital gain from the sale. Since his basis in the stock is the same as his mother's, Bill's holding period in the stock includes the time that his mother held the stock. Therefore, Bill would be deemed to have held the stock more than 12 months, even though he actually owned the stock less than one month. Because he is in the 15% tax bracket, his maximum capital gains tax on the $5,000 gain would be $250 ($5,000 x 5%). There has been an overall reduction of $500 in federal income tax because Judy made a gift of the stock instead of selling it and making a gift of the proceeds.

Planning Alert If you are interested in helping a child or grandchild with future college costs, your ability to shift your capital gains tax by making a gift takes on even more significance. For example, assume grandparents gift stock or mutual funds to their grandchild in 2005 when the child is 14 years old. If the grandchild sells the asset to help pay college costs and is in the 10% tax bracket in the year of the sale, the maximum long-term capital gains rate would be 5%. The tax savings could be dramatic if the grandchild sells the gifted stock in 2008 when the zero-percent rate is scheduled to replace the 5% rate. The sale of the asset would, at least in part, not be taxed at all.

Capital Gains and Inherited Property

When an individual inherits property from a decedent, the individual is generally able to have any gain from the sale of the property classified as a long-term capital gain. Thus, the tax that results from the sale of the property cannot exceed that computed under the maximum long-term capital gains rate (i.e., 15%). This is because Code Sec. 1223(11) provides that, in most situations, the individual who receives the property from a decedent will be considered to have held the property "for more than one year."

Example On January 3, 2005, Steven Martin inherits 100 shares of Surprise Inc. from his Uncle Jack. Steven's basis in the stock is equal to the fair market value of the shares at the date of his uncle's death, $5,000. Steven sells the shares on January 7, 2005, for $6,000. Even though he only owed the stock a few days, Steven's $1,000 gain is treated as long-term because he is deemed to have held the inherited shares "more than one year." As a result, his tax on the $1,000 gain is computed by using the maximum long-term capital gains rate of 15% (or 5% if Steven is in the 10% or 15% tax bracket).

Additional Capital Gains Considerations

Although it is always important to keep the holding period for long-term capital gains in mind, there are a number of other specialized rules that may also come into play when you make your investment decisions for 2005 and beyond. The following is an overview of some of these additional considerations:

    (1)   *Collectibles.* If you hold certain "collectibles" for more than 12 months, any gain will be taxed at a maximum capital gains rate of 28%. Gain from collectibles does not qualify for the lowest capital gains rate of 15% even if you hold them for more than 12 months.

Gain will be taxed as ordinary income when you hold a collectible for 12 months or less. The term "collectibles" generally includes such items as works of art, antiques, rugs, gems, stamps, gold, silver, and platinum bullion and coins.

(2)   *Alternative Minimum Tax*. If you are liable for the alternative minimum tax (AMT), your AMT will be calculated by using the same capital gains rates that are used to compute your regular income tax. In short, you will not be put at a disadvantage for AMT purposes just because you have long-term capital gains.

(3)   *Mutual Funds and Other Pass-Through Entities*. The favorable capital gains rate applies to long-term capital gains distributed by certain pass-through entities (e.g., mutual funds, real estate investment trusts and S corporations). The entity is required to inform the taxpayer concerning the proper classification of distributions (e.g., short-term or long-term).

(4)   *District of Columbia and Renewal Communities Tax Incentives*. There are enhanced tax incentives for investing in businesses located within the District of Columbia Enterprise Zone and "renewal communities." Among these incentives is a zero capital gains rate for gain from certain assets that have been held for more than five years.

(5)   *Small Business Stock*. Individuals may elect to rollover capital gain from the sale of qualifying small business stock held for more than six months if other small business stock is purchased during the 60-day period beginning on the date of sale. For additional tax incentives, see "Investment in Qualified Small Businesses," below.

(6)   *Like-Kind Exchanges*. If you exchange business or investment property for other business or investment property of a like-kind, you do not pay tax on any gain or deduct any loss until you sell or dispose of the property you receive. To be nontaxable, a trade must meet a number of special rules including timing issues and identification requirements. The like-kind exchange rules do not extend to property you use for personal purposes (e.g., your home or family car).

(7)   *Sale of Principal Residence*. For many individuals, their biggest investment takes the form of their principal residence. Homeowners may be able to sell their principal residences and not have to pay any federal income tax on their realized gain. Ownership and use requirements must be met and the exclusion may not be used more frequently than once every two years. A married couple may exclude up to $500,000 of gain. A $250,000 exclusion applies to unmarried individuals. See page 58.

Tax Tip If you are thinking about selling a mutual fund in 2005, when determining your potential capital gain or loss, don't forget to add all your reinvested interest, dividends, capital gains distributions, and sales charges to your original cost basis. By including these already-taxed items of income into your basis, your taxable gain will be reduced, or your deductible loss will be increased.

Timing Decisions

One of the greatest areas of investment planning flexibility comes from your ability to time your investment transactions for maximum tax benefit. Often the change of a few days in the timing of sales or acquisitions of stocks or bonds can make a significant difference in the way a transaction is taxed. When the end of the year approaches, you should add up all the gains and losses you have realized to date and compare them with the unrealized gains and losses in your portfolio. When making an investment decision, economic factors in the market should take priority over tax considerations. You should not hold on to an asset just because you don't want to pay tax on the gain. Conversely, you should not sell an asset just to take a tax loss if you think that the asset will rise in value. After considering the economic factors, you should consider the tax minimizing strategies discussed below.

Capital gains are especially fertile areas for planning because you typically have greater control over when the income is realized than you do over your salary, business income, and interest and dividend income. In most situations, you have the power to determine when your gains and/or losses will be recognized for income tax purposes. In making an informed decision, you must know the rules governing the deduction of capital losses. Your net capital losses are deductible on a dollar-for-dollar basis against net capital gains. Excess losses are allowed to offset up to $3,000 of ordinary income ($1,500 if you are married and filing separately). Losses remaining after the limit may be carried forward indefinitely. Basic timing decisions include the use of the following strategies:

(1) Sell capital gain property before the end of 2005 if you have already realized capital losses for the year that exceed the sum of any capital gains you have already realized plus $3,000 ($1,500 if you are married and filing separately).

(2) If you have an excess of gains over losses, sell loss property to offset the excess gains and eliminate the tax on them.

(3) If your other allowable deductions for 2005 exceed your income, you should avoid realizing any further capital losses in 2005. Additional loss deductions would be valueless in 2005. Furthermore, the excess non-capital loss deductions may not be eligible to be carried over to a later year and would, therefore, be wasted.

(4)   If you need to raise cash before the end of the year, loss property should be sold before property in which you have a gain. Conversely, if you only have gain property, sell long-term property before short-term property in order to take advantage of the special tax rates on long-term gains (i.e., 15% or 5%).

Wash Sales

On occasion you may want to recognize a loss for tax purposes on a stock or security without completely abandoning your investment position. One technique for maintaining your continuity in the investment is to sell the loss security and, within a short time after or before the sale, you reacquire the same security.

However, the "wash sale" rule imposes time limits on the sale and repurchase of the same securities. If these time limits are violated, you will not be able to claim your loss in the year of sale. The wash sale rule comes into play when you sell or exchange securities at a loss and within 30 days before of after the sale you:

(1)   buy substantially identical stock or securities;
(2)   acquire substantially identical stock or securities in a fully taxable trade; or
(3)   acquire a contract or option to buy substantially identical stock or securities.

Tax Tip   Even if you violate the wash sale time limits, the loss that you cannot currently deduct is not permanently lost. Instead the disallowed loss is added to the cost of the new stock or securities you purchased. Your holding period for the new stock or securities includes the period of time that you held the stock or securities that you sold.

Example   On December 10, 2004, Erik Anderson purchased 100 shares of Xymet, Inc. stock for $1,000. On December 15, 2005, he sold these shares for $750 and on December 20, 2005, he purchased 100 shares of Xymet for $800. Under the wash sale rule, Erik cannot deduct his loss of $250 on his 2005 tax return. However, he may add the disallowed loss of $250 to the cost of the new stock, $800, to obtain his basis in the new stock, which is $1,050 ($800 cost plus $250 unallowed wash sale loss). His holding period for the stock purchased on December 20, 2005, includes his holding period for the stock purchased on December 10, 2004.

Techniques that you may use to avoid the loss limits imposed by the wash sale rule include:

(1) Wait at least 31 days before purchasing substantially identical stock or securities. The risk inherent in using this technique is that you lose out on any gain on the stock that may occur during the waiting period.

(2) "Double up," that is, buy a second lot that is equal to the original holding, wait 31 days, and then sell the original lot, thereby recognizing the loss. This allows you to maintain a continuing interest in the stock. However, you have to tie up additional funds for at least 31 days to accomplish your goal and you double your downside risk.

(3) Sell the loss stock and reinvest in the stock of another company in the same industry that has historically performed the same way as the loss stock. After 31 days, you can reverse the process to restore your original holding. This method minimizes your risk during the waiting period and you do not violate the wash sale rule because the stocks of two different companies are not considered to be substantially identical.

 Planning Alert In determining whether stock or securities are substantially identical, all the facts and circumstances must be considered. Generally, stocks or securities of one corporation are not considered substantially identical to stocks or securities of another corporation. Bonds or preferred stock of a corporation are not ordinarily considered substantially identical to the common stock of the same corporation.

Mutual Funds: Recordkeeping is Key

Before planning your mutual fund investment strategy for year-end 2005, and for 2006, it is vital that you establish a system of recordkeeping. Doing so will likely save you tax dollars, as well as headaches when it comes time to report the transactions. Seemingly inconsequential activities (e.g., writing a check against your mutual fund account, making a phone call to transfer money into a new fund, or reinvesting your dividends and capital gains distributions) will have significant tax and compliance implications. Carefully maintained records are crucial to establishing a basis, determining holding period, and avoiding the wash sale limits. Fortunately, many mutual funds and brokerage firms now maintain detailed records concerning your account and can provide the information you need in some of these areas. However, in the event these records are not maintained or not available, you will have to depend on your own records.

If you have elected to have mutual fund dividends and capital gain distributions automatically reinvested, you need to retain all fund transaction statements, or periodical statements, to ensure that when you sell the shares, you do not understate your basis, and effectively be taxed twice on the reinvested income. In addition, without careful planning and recordkeeping, you may unwittingly run afoul of the wash sale rules by selling mutual fund shares at a loss within 30 days of an automatic dividend reinvestment.

It is also important to keep track of any checks drawn on your mutual fund account. Each withdrawal is really a taxable transaction involving the redemption of mutual fund shares. Every check withdrawal must be reported on Schedule D as a separate transaction. Transferring money between different mutual funds has become increasingly easier, and can be accomplished by a quick phone call or a visit to a web site. Keep in mind, however, that unless you are moving money between mutual funds within or between retirement plan accounts, the transfer is a taxable transaction that must be reported on Schedule D.

Thus, when you begin planning any mutual fund sales, make sure that you have the necessary records covering such items as dates of purchase, reinvestment amounts, and prior sales so that you are able to make an informed and tax-wise decision concerning your planned sale.

Investment in Qualified Small Businesses

There is a substantial tax advantage for individuals who invest in certain small businesses that operate in the corporate form. The tax advantage allows an investor to exclude 50% of the gain realized from the sale of qualified small business stock. Among the many requirements that have to be met in order for the exclusion to apply are that the stock has to be held by the investor for at least five years and the investor must have acquired the stock at its original issue. This rule applies to stock issued after August 10, 1993, by a C corporation that operates an active business and has less than $50 million in gross assets.

However, the maximum capital gains rate of 15% does not apply to the portion of the gain that is included in the investor's income. Instead, a maximum tax rate of 28% applies to the 50% of the gain that is included in income. As a result of the 50% exclusion, the investor's total gain from a qualified investment is actually subject to a maximum effective tax rate of only 14% (i.e., 50% recognized gain x 28% maximum tax rate). The gain that may be excludable by an investor on the stock from one issuer cannot exceed the greater of: (1) 10 times the taxpayer's basis in the stock; or (2) $10 million gain from stock in that corporation.

Example On November 1, 1995, Al Sloop invested $5,000 in newly issued qualified small business stock. He sold the stock on December 1, 2005, for $11,000. Al can exclude $3,000 of his total realized gain ($6,000 x 50%) from his gross income. His recognized gain of $3,000 can not be taxed at a rate that exceeds 28%. If Al's marginal tax rate is under 28% (e.g., 25%), his income tax on the gain would be computed by applying that lower rate.

 Tax Alert Effective for dispositions of small business stock on or after May 6, 2003, only 7% of the 50% is treated as a tax preference item when computing alternative minimum taxable income (AMTI). As a result, 3.5% (50% x 7%) of an investor's total gain from the sale of small business stock will be used in the computation of AMTI.

The stock of certain corporations can never qualify under this exclusion provision. For example, if the principal asset of a corporation is the skill of one or more of its employees, its stock will not qualify. Examples of these excluded corporations are those engaged in providing health, legal, engineering, or accounting services. Also excluded are corporations involved in banking, investing or farming, or in the hotel, motel or restaurant industry.

 Planning Alert Potential investors in such stock should factor into their investment decision the possibility that if the corporation is a new "start-up" business, the chance for capital loss may be greater than the potential for capital gain. However, even if this is the case, the possibility that any resultant capital gain could be taxed at a maximum of 14% may outweigh the risk to investment capital. In addition, an investor may elect to roll over gain from the sale of small business stock held for more than 6 months if other small business stock is purchased during the 60-day period beginning on the date of sale.

Investment in Small Business Investment Companies

Another significant tax advantage is offered to investors in common stock or partnership interests of a specialized small business investment company (SSBIC). An SSBIC is one that is licensed by the Small Business Administration. Its investments are directed toward businesses owned by socially or economically disadvantaged persons.

Investors who sell publicly traded stock and use the proceeds to buy an interest in an SSBIC can elect to defer taxation on any gain realized from the sale of the stock. The gain would be rolled over into the SSBIC and would reduce the investor's basis. In the case of SSBIC stock, the investor's basis is not reduced for purposes of calculating the gain eligible for the 50% exclusion that now applies to investments in certain small business stock (see above). The amount of gain that an individual can elect to roll over is limited to a yearly maximum of $50,000 and a lifetime cap of $500,000 ($25,000 and $250,000, respectively, for married individuals filing separately). Corporate investors are subject to a yearly maximum rollover of $250,000 and a lifetime cap of $1,000,000.

Tax-Exempt Bonds

As part of an overall investment strategy that is directed toward enhancing returns and lowering income taxes, individuals should consider whether tax-exempt bonds should play a role in their investment portfolio. Although the nominal interest rate on tax-exempt bonds is generally lower than that offered by taxable bonds with a comparable quality and maturity, the after-tax yield from the tax-exempt bond may well be higher. Ideally, an individual should invest in bonds that are exempt from federal and state income taxes.

The following chart shows the yields that an individual would have to receive from an investment that produces taxable interest in order to match yields that are exempt from federal tax.

Equivalent Taxable
Rates Based on Tax-Free Rate of:
Interest Rates

Tax Rates	2%	3%	4%	5%	6%	7%	8%
10%	2.22%	3.33%	4.44%	5.56%	6.67%	7.78%	8.89%
15%	2.35%	3.53%	4.71%	5.88%	7.06%	8.24%	9.41%
25%	2.67%	4.00%	5.33%	6.66%	8.00%	9.33%	10.66%
28%	2.78%	4.17%	5.56%	6.94%	8.33%	9.72%	11.11%
33%	2.99%	4.48%	5.97%	7.46%	8.95%	10.44%	11.94%
35%	3.08%	4.62%	6.15%	7.69%	9.23%	10.77%	12.31%

The equivalent taxable yields in the table are computed by dividing the tax-exempt interest rate by the difference between one and the tax bracket rate. For example, the table shows that the equivalent taxable yield is 10.44% for a taxpayer in the 33% tax bracket if the tax-exempt yield is 7%. The equivalent taxable yield is computed as follows: .07/(1 - .33) = .1044 or 10.44%.

Example For 2005, Ruth Thorton is in the 35% tax bracket. She has the choice of purchasing a $10,000 bond with a taxable yield of 5% or a tax-exempt bond with a yield of 4%. In order to minimize her 2005 federal income tax, Ruth's wisest choice would be to purchase the tax-exempt bond. Even though the tax-exempt yield is less than that offered by the taxable bond, she would be obtaining an equivalent taxable yield of 6.15% from the tax-exempt bond.

Of course, you have to look at more than a comparison of tax-exempt and taxable yields.

The credit risk inherent in the purchase of any debt must be carefully considered. If you are retired and receiving Social Security benefits, the fact that tax-exempt interest has to be taken into account when determining the taxable portion of your Social Security benefits should also enter into your decision-making process.

Sale of Principal Residence

Individuals may elect to exclude from income up to $250,000 of gain realized from the sale of a principal residence. For married individuals, the maximum exclusion available is $500,000. The gain exclusion is a powerful tax/retirement savings device in an environment in which housing costs appreciate over the years. Like a Roth IRA, from which withdrawals of earnings are tax free, the exclusion allows you to withdraw the appreciation from your home tax-free when you sell it.

In order to be eligible for the exclusion, the individual must have owned and occupied the home as a principal residence for at least two years of the five year period that ends on the date of sale. Married couples may use the $500,000 amount if: (1) either spouse meets the ownership test; (2) both spouses meet the use test; (3) neither spouse is ineligible for the exclusion by virtue of a sale or exchange of a principal residence within the last two years; and (4) the couple files a joint tax return for the year of sale.

Tax Tip Even if you do not satisfy the ownership and use requirements mentioned above, you still might be eligible to exclude a portion of your gain. This partial exclusion applies if you sold your home due to: (1) a change in your place of employment; (2) health reasons; or (3) unforeseen circumstances (e.g., divorce or loss of employment).

If you were entitled to take depreciation deductions because you used your home for business purposes or as rental property, you cannot exclude the part of your gain equal to any depreciation allowed or allowable as a deduction for periods after May 6, 1997. However, if you can show the IRS that the depreciation deduction you claimed was less than the amount that was allowable, the amount you cannot exclude cannot exceed the amount you claimed. For example, if you were entitled to claim depreciation because you had a home office, but you can show that you never claimed a depreciation deduction, your exclusion would not be reduced.

If you are married and your spouse dies, special considerations may come into play if you and your spouse owned the house jointly. You are entitled to the $500,000 exclusion if you sell your residence in the year of the spouse's death. But if you wait until the following year or later to sell, the $250,000 exclusion applies (assuming that you haven't remarried). The tax cost of losing one-half of the $500,000 exclusion could be as high as $37,500 ($250,000 x 15% capital gains rate). The decision to sell in the year of your spouse's death in order to take advantage of the full $500,000 exclusion, however, needs to be evaluated in light of the basis step-up rule which is discussed in the following material.

If you are a surviving spouse and you owned your home jointly, your basis in the home will change. The new basis for the half interest that your spouse owned will be 50% of the fair market value on the date of death (or alternate valuation date). The basis in your half of the home will remain at 50% of the adjusted basis determined previously. As a surviving spouse, your new basis in your home is the total of these two amounts.

Example   Mary Smith and her husband Bob purchased their jointly owned home a few years ago for $150,000. Bob died in 2005. The fair market value of their home at the time of his death was $200,000. Mary's new basis in the home is $175,000 ($75,000, one-half of their original adjusted basis, plus $100,000, one-half of fair market value at time of Bob's death). If Mary sells the home in 2006 for $275,000, her realized gain would be $100,000. Because she is entitled to exclude up to $250,000 of gain, no portion of her gain would be included in her income.

Tax Alert   If you are a resident of a community property state (i.e., Arizona, California, Idaho, Louisiana, Nevada, New Mexico, Texas, Washington, and Wisconsin), you are subject to somewhat different rules when determining your basis. Please consult your tax advisor.

Planning Alert   Since Congress amended the rules for home office deductions for tax years beginning after 1998, more small business owners with home offices have been able to deduct their trade or business expenses. This is because the change expanded the definition of principal place of business. A home office will qualify as a taxpayer's principal place of business if: (1) the office is used by the taxpayer to conduct administrative or management activities of the trade or business; and (2) there is no other fixed location of the trade or business where the taxpayer conducts substantial administrative or management activities.

Caution! The expanded definition does not affect the requirement that home office expenses are deductible only if the office is used by the taxpayer exclusively on a regular basis as a place of business. Also, if the taxpayer is an employee, the taxpayer's use of the home office must be for the convenience of the employer. In addition, if the taxpayer is planning on selling his or her home, consideration should be given to the adverse effect that a home office deduction may have on the availability of the exclusion of gain on the sale of the home. For a discussion of these home office implications, see page 128.

Sale of Vacation Home

If you own a vacation home as well as a principal residence, with careful planning you will be able to have the exclusion apply to both of your homes. In order to achieve this significant tax benefit, after you sell your principal residence and claim the allowable exclusion permitted for that property, you must take all necessary steps to establish your former vacation home as your new principal residence. The IRS uses a facts and circumstances test when it determines if a former vacation home was actually converted into a new principal residence. Because there are no hard and fast rules that you can depend upon to help establish the conversion, you should build as strong a case as possible. This would include taking such steps as:

(1)   being able to prove that you resided in the home for at least two years;
(2)   registering to vote in the area where the home is located;
(3)   notify the IRS of your new address by filing Form 8822, "Change of Address;"
(4)   filing your state, local and federal tax returns from your new address;
(5)   having all mail (e.g., checking account statement and credit card bills) sent to your new home; and
(6)   registering your cars with the proper state and/or local authorities.

   The value of vacation homes in some parts of the country has increased significantly over the past years. If you find yourself in this fortunate position, you may be able to reap the tax-free benefit of the home exclusion provision when you sell your "former vacation home" a few years after you sell your former principal residence.

Retirement Planning

Your 2005 tax planning is not complete without a re-view of the retirement plan options that are available to you. Decisions you make in 2005 not only affect your current and future tax liabilities, but also impact the amount of assets that you will have available during your retirement years.

Over the past few years, retirement planning has taken on added levels of complexity due to the many options that are now available to you. These options include yearly increases in the maximum amount that you may contribute to various retirement plans, special "catch-up" contributions if you are over age 49, and the liberalization of the rollover rules between different types of plans. In addition, you may now have the option of contributing to a traditional IRA or a Roth IRA. Each type of IRA offers its own unique tax benefits. Both traditional and Roth IRAs are discussed below under "Benefiting from IRAs."

Before You Retire

Participation in an employer pension or profit-shar-ing plan, a 401(k) plan, a Keogh plan, a simplified employee pension (SEP) or an IRA adds flexibility to your tax planning in the following ways:

Reducing your 2005 tax. A contribution to a deductible retirement plan reduces your adjusted gross income (AGI) by the amount of the contribu-tion (within specified limits). Thus, deductible re-tirement plan contributions will reduce your current income tax. The earnings on money in a retirement account are not currently taxed and, as a result, your retirement plan assets grow at a faster pace than assets that are not in a tax-deferred account. Generally, the funds will be subject to tax when you withdraw them, but you may be in a much lower bracket at that time. Remember that contributions to a Roth IRA do not reduce AGI.

If eligible, you can get a tax credit of up to $1,000 ($2,000 if filing jointly). This is called the Retirement Contributions Savings Credit. Without future Congres-sional action, this credit will not be available after 2005.

To qualify for the credit, you must meet certain requirements. You must be at least 18 years old and not be a full-time student. No one else can be claiming you as an exemption (your parents for example). Your AGI must be below a certain level depending on your filing status. If you are married filing jointly, AGI cannot be more than $50,000. If you file as head of household, AGI cannot be more than $37,500. If you file single, married filing separately, or qualifying widow(er) with dependent child, AGI cannot be more than $25,000.

Contributions that are eligible for the credit are contributions to a traditional or Roth IRA, and salary reduction deferrals including a 401(k) plan, 403(b) annuity, governmental 457 plan, a SIMPLE, or a SEP. Voluntary after-tax contributions to a qualified retirement plan or 403(b) annuity are also eligible. In computing the credit, eligible contributions are reduced by distributions received during the test period. The test period ends on the due date of the return (including extensions) and looks back to the current tax year and the two previous tax years. For your 2005 tax return, assuming you have a calendar tax year, this would generally mean a test period starting January 2003 and ending on the due date of your return (April 17, 2006 (April 15, 2006, is a Saturday)).

 Tax Tip Even if you don't receive a deduction or credit for your retirement plan contribution, you still obtain a tax savings because the income or gain that you realize in your retirement plan will be tax deferred. You also achieve the desirable result of having the retirement plan's income or gain grow on a tax-deferred basis over a long period of time.

Source of funds. Most retirement plan contributions reduce your current liquidity. Even though you legally "own" the funds, you rarely have immediate access to them. If you have a vested interest in an employer-sponsored plan, you can often ease the liquidity problem related to income deferral by borrowing from the plan. Many plans are set up so that the interest you pay on such a loan goes to the benefit of your account. This provides you a way to access your retirement funds without paying too great a cost.

Pre-retirement withdrawals. Generally, there is a 10% penalty on withdrawals made before you reach the age of 59½. However, in an emergency situation, the 10% penalty may not be that great a deterrent to obtaining the needed funds. For example, assume you are in the 15% bracket this year and you need the funds for an emergency, you can withdraw the needed funds at a tax rate of 25% (15% bracket plus 10% penalty). If you have no income tax liability for the year, you will be able to obtain the funds and only be responsible for the 10% penalty. Of course, the purpose of the retirement account is to help you provide for your retirement. Funds should only be withdrawn as a last resort.

The good news is that the 10% penalty does not apply to all distributions made before you are age 59 ½. Among the withdrawals that you may make without paying the 10% penalty are those: (1) due to your disability; (2) made in the form of certain periodic payments over your life or the joint lives of you and your beneficiary; or (3) used to pay medical expenses in excess of 7.5% of adjusted gross income.

Tax Tip Distributions from a traditional IRA are not subject to the 10% tax on early (pre-age 59½) withdrawals if you use the amounts to: (1) pay qualified higher education expenses; (2) pay expenses incurred for qualified first-time home buying expenses (up to a $10,000 lifetime limit); or (3) purchase health insurance of an unemployed individual if certain conditions are met.

When to retire. Recent years have seen steady erosion of the tax benefits available for distributions from employer-sponsored retirement plans. First came an elimination of capital gain treatment. Then came a change from 10-year to five-year averaging for lump-sum distributions. Subsequently, the five-year averaging was repealed. Although these changes are typically put into force on a delayed basis to avoid harm to individuals who are soon to retire, these types of delays are not required and may not be adopted in the future. If you expect to retire in the next few years, you should keep track of Congressional action. Depending on the change, an early retirement could save you from additional taxes that would otherwise be due because of an expiring tax benefit.

Tax Tip The 10-year averaging method remains in effect for individuals who attained age 50 before January 1, 1986. Of course, current taxation can be avoided by using the option to rollover the distribution into a traditional IRA or another employer plan that accepts these rollovers.

After You Retire

Among the tax planning options that you should consider after you retire are:

Distribution or rollover. Retirees often have a wide variety of options on how to receive benefits from their retirement plans: periodic payments, annuities, lump-sum distributions, or combinations of these. Each has its own tax consequences. Projecting your financial needs and your tax situation several years into the future must be done when determining which option is best for you.

Withholding on distributions. If you receive a lump-sum distribution from a pension or profit sharing plan, you generally will be subject to a 20% withholding tax. The withholding tax can be avoided only if the distribution is transferred directly to another retirement plan, including a traditional IRA. If you do not arrange a direct transfer and instead receive the distribution yourself, the 20% will be withheld from the distribution even if you meet the 60-day rollover rules. This means that you will have to come up with funds from another source if you want to roll over the full amount of the distribution. However, you will recover the 20% that was withheld when you file your return for the year of the distribution, either as a refund or as a payment toward your total income tax liability.

Post-retirement IRAs. The fact that you have retired does not mean you have to stop contributing to an IRA. For 2005 and 2006, you may contribute the lesser of $4,000 or 100 percent of your earned income for the year, the same as before your retirement. The contribution limit increases to $5,000 in 2008 and later years. If you are at least 50 years old by the end of the year, you will be able to make an additional catch-up contribution of $500 for 2005. In 2006 and later years, the catch-up contribution increases to $1,000. Obviously, if you are not working at all, you don't meet the earned income requirement, but you only need minimal earnings from a part-time job in order to obtain the tax benefits of an IRA. However, you cannot make contributions to a traditional IRA for the year in which you reach age 70½ or any later years. Roth IRA contributions may be made no matter how old you are.

 Tax Tip If your adjusted gross income is low enough to allow you to make contributions to a traditional IRA as well as your employer's retirement plan and you can only afford to make contributions to one of the plans, contribute to the employer plan if the employer provides matching contributions. An IRA, however, does give you more flexibility in directing the way in which your contributions are invested.

Benefiting from IRAs

For 2005, you may be able to contribute $4,000 to a traditional IRA or a Roth IRA. In some situations you may find it desirable to allocate the $4,000 between a traditional IRA and a Roth IRA. If you are at least 50-years old by the end of the year, you can make a "catch-up" contribution of $500.

 Tax Tip If you are under age 50, you may contribute a maximum combined total of $4,000 to all your IRAs for 2005. If you find that your maximum deductible contribution to a traditional IRA is $1,000, you will generally be able to contribute an additional $3,000 to a Roth IRA. This technique will allow you to combine your maximum deduction with your maximum contribution. You may not contribute $4,000 to your traditional IRA and another $4,000 to your Roth IRA for any tax year.

 **Planning Alert** Your 2005 contribution to a traditional and/or Roth IRA may be deposited up to April 17, 2006 (April 15, 2006, is a Saturday). This is one of the few steps you can take to reduce your 2005 tax after the year ends. April 17, 2006, is the final date even if you have obtained an extension to file your 2005 tax return.

For 2005, an individual who is under age 70½ may be able to deduct contributions to a traditional IRA up to the lesser of $4,000 ($4,500 if age 50 or older) or 100% of compensation. The $4,000 deduction is phased out if the individual: (1) is an active participant in an employer's retirement plan for any part of a year; and (2) has modified adjusted gross income (MAGI) in excess of a specific amount. The applicable MAGI limits depend upon the individual's filing status and the limits will be increased annually over the next few years. Modified AGI for this purpose is adjusted gross income without taking into account the exclusions for educational U.S. savings bonds, employer paid adoption assistance, student loan interest, qualified tuition expenses, foreign earned income and housing, or the IRA deduction itself.

The following chart shows the deduction phaseout limits that are generally applied for 2005.

Traditional IRA Deduction Phaseout for 2005

Filing status	Full deduction if your MAGI is:	Partial deduction if your MAGI is:	No deduction if your MAGI is:
Single (including head of household)	$50,000 or less	$50,001 to $60,000	$60,001 and above
Married filing jointly	$70,000 or less	$70,001 to $80,000	$80,001 and above
Married filing separately	N/A	$0 to $10,000	$10,001 and above

Individuals may make nondeductible contributions to a traditional IRA to the extent that deductible contributions are disallowed due to the MAGI phaseout limits. However, if you are in this situation, you should consider the advantages of making the nondeductible contribution to a Roth IRA instead of the traditional IRA.

Tax Tip An individual is not considered an active participant in an employer-sponsored plan merely because the individual's spouse is an active participant for any part of a plan year. This allows more individuals to take a full deduction for a contribution to a traditional IRA, even if their spouse is covered under a retirement plan at work. However, the maximum deductible IRA contribution for the spouse who is not an active participant, but whose spouse is, is phased out for a MAGI between $150,000 and $160,000 (jointly computed). No deduction is permitted if their joint MAGI is over $160,000.

Example Bob is covered by a 401(k) plan sponsored by his employer. His wife, Betty, age 45, is not employed. The couple files a joint income tax return for 2005, with a modified adjusted gross income of $120,000. Betty may make a $4,000 deductible contribution to a traditional IRA for 2005 because she is not an active participant in an employer-sponsored retirement plan and their combined MAGI is below $150,000. However, Bob may not make a deductible IRA contribution because their combined MAGI is above the phaseout range for active participants who are married and filing jointly ($70,000 to $80,000 for 2005).

Example Assume the same facts as above, except that the couple's MAGI was $200,000 for 2005. Neither Bob nor Betty would be able to make a deductible contribution to a traditional IRA because their combined MAGI was over $160,000.

Roth IRAs

A Roth IRA may be an alternative to the traditional IRA. The Roth IRA is funded using nondeductible contributions. If you meet specific requirements, the interest, dividends and appreciation that accrues in your Roth IRA are not subject to federal income tax when funds are withdrawn. Your maximum 2005 contribution to both types of IRAs is limited to $4,000 ($4,500 if you are at least 50 years old). Unlike traditional IRAs, you may make contributions to a Roth IRA after you reach 70½ and you do not have to withdraw Roth IRA funds during your lifetime.

As with traditional IRAs, your ability to make Roth IRA contributions is subject to income limits. The maximum yearly contribution that can be made to a Roth IRA is phased out for single taxpayers with modified adjusted gross income (MAGI) between $95,000 and $110,000, for joint filers with

MAGI between $150,000 and $160,000, and for married filing separately with MAGI between $0 and $10,000.

 Tax Tip In order to obtain the tax-free benefits that a Roth IRA has to offer, a distribution must be "qualified." To be "qualified" the distribution must satisfy a five-year holding period and must meet one of the following four requirements. The distribution must be made: (1) after the individual attains age 59½; (2) to a beneficiary on or after the individual's death; (3) because of the individual's disability; or (4) to pay for certain first-time home buying expenses.

Contribution and Deferral Limitations

The annual amount that you can contribute each year to an IRA, a 401(k) plan, 403(b) annuities, 457 plan, or SIMPLE plan is subject to adjustment over the next few years. The IRA contribution limit ($4,000 in 2005 for traditional and Roth IRAs) increases to $5,000 in 2008, and will be adjusted for inflation after 2008. The limit for 401(k), 403(b), and 457 plans ($14,000 in 2005) increases to $15,000 in 2006, and is subject to inflation adjustment in 2007 and later years. The contribution limit for SIMPLE plans ($10,000 in 2005) will be adjusted for inflation in 2006 and later years.

 Tax Tip If you participate in a 457 plan, your elective deferral limit is twice the otherwise applicable limit in the three years prior to your retirement.

Catch-up Contributions. Another important benefit allows you to make additional "catch-up" contributions to your retirement plan if you are at least 50 years old by the end of the tax year. Individuals are allowed to contribute these extra amounts to all types of retirement plans, including IRAs and 401(k) plans. You should carefully evaluate your financial situation to see if you can take advantage of catch-up contributions in order to reduce your current taxable income and/or set aside more money for retirement.

Maximum Catch-Up Contributions to Various Retirement Plans

Tax Year	IRA	401(k), 403(b), and 457 plans	SIMPLE plans
2005	$500	$4,000	$2,000
2006	$1,000	$5,000	$2,500
2007	$1,000	$5,000*	$2,500

* Subject to annual inflation adjustment

Rollovers from Traditional IRAs to Roth IRAs

You may be eligible to rollover funds from a traditional IRA into a Roth IRA. However, the rollover is treated as a taxable event and you will be treated as if you had received a distribution from the traditional IRA. The total taxable amount is included in your income in the year the rollover took place. Penalties will not be applied if requirements are met. The reason for making the rollover is to convert money from a tax-deferred account into an account that offers tax-free withdrawals. Future earnings and growth generated by the Roth IRA will escape further taxation.

You will be able to make the rollover if for the year of transfer: (1) your AGI does not exceed $100,000; and (2) you are not married filing separately.

Your decision whether to convert a traditional IRA into a Roth IRA can only be made after a careful evaluation of all the various tax and investment factors that come into play. Among these factors are: (1) the total income tax you will pay because of the conversion; (2) the costs you will incur because of the conversion (e.g., transaction fees and sales charges); (3) your anticipated tax bracket when you would have received distributions from the traditional IRA; (4) the anticipated return from the Roth and traditional IRA; (5) your age at the time of conversion; and (6) the length of time it will take you to recoup the tax and other expenses caused by the conversion. Your tax or investment advisor should be consulted before you make the Roth conversion.

 Tax Tip You may participate in an employer's qualified retirement plan and also make maximum contributions to a Roth IRA if your income does not exceed yearly limits. For example, Roth contributions are phased out for joint filers when their MAGI is between $150,000 and $160,000. Roth contributions are phased out for single filers with a MAGI between $95,000 and $110,000.

Keogh Plans

If you have net earnings from self-employment, you may be eligible to open and contribute to a special retirement plan for self-employed individuals. This special retirement plan is referred to as a Keogh plan. You do not have to carry on a full-time business activity in order to be considered self-employed. Thus, if you work for a salary during the day and conduct a business from your home in the evenings, the net earnings from your home business are considered self-employment income.

Although contributions and deductions for a self-employed person covered by a qualified plan are subject to the same basic rules as participants who are employees, there are special rules to be considered. For a discussion of plans covering self-employed individuals, see page 130.

 Tax Tip Keogh plans, and some other types of retirement plans must be established by the end of your tax year (e.g., December 31, 2005). However, you may fund the Keogh plan for the prior year up to the due date of your return for that year, including filing extensions. For example, if you requested a four-month filing extension to file your tax return, you generally have until August 15, 2006, to make your 2005 Keogh plan contribution.

 Planning Alert Recent changes in the tax law have made it advantageous for small business owners who have no employees (other than a spouse) to set up a Code Sec. 401(k) plan. One-person 401(k) plans, which are often referred to as "self-employed 401(k)," "solo 401(k)," or "individual 401(k)" plans, allow a sole owner to make greater tax-deferred and tax-deductible contributions than would be permitted under a Keogh. At this time, this type of retirement plan does not appear to be sponsored by very many brokerage firms or other types of financial institutions. However, if you are interested in maximizing your retirement plan contributions based on your self-employment income you should investigate the pros and cons of this type of retirement plan.

Employer-Sponsored Plans

Most companies permit employees to earmark a percentage of their salary to a 401(k), up to the annual dollar limit set by law ($14,000 for 2005, plus a $4,000 catch-up contribution, if you are eligible). The rules governing employer-sponsored plans are quite complicated. For your tax planning purposes, you should know:

- how your plan operates and the limits on the amounts you may contribute to the plan (if any);
- how your employer's contribution is computed;
- whether you may direct the investment of your account;
- whether you have the option of either receiving the employer's contribution in cash when it is made or letting money go into the plan (a 401(k) plan);
- whether you can borrow from the fund; and
- how and when you can begin withdrawing from the fund.

If you are entitled to make contributions to a 401(k) plan, the tax benefits of a 401(k) are generally more significant than those associated with a traditional IRA. For example, your maximum contributions to a 401(k) are larger, your employer may match a portion of your contributions, and if needed, you may be able to borrow some of the money in your 401(k).

In addition to providing retirement benefits, the 401(k) plan may be a source of funds. If certain rules are followed you may be able to borrow from your 401(k) account balance. As long as your loan does not exceed the *lesser* of: (1) $50,000; or (2) the *larger* of $10,000 or 50% of your accrued benefits under the plan, the loan will not be treated as a taxable distribution. Generally, the loan must be repaid within five years. There is an exception for home loans. Loans in excess of the specified amounts or that have longer repayment periods are treated as taxable distributions.

Tax Tip It is important to be aware of the tax consequences of an outstanding 401(k) plan loan balance if you are planning to leave your employer. If your loans are not paid off by the termination of employment, before you can rollover your plan proceeds, your employer will reduce or offset your vested 401(k) plan benefit by the unpaid balance of the loan. This offset is considered a distribution, and you will be required to include it in your gross income. Even if your employer's plan gives you the option of staying with the 401(k) plan after employment is terminated, most plans require that loans be repaid within a relatively short period of time after termination (e.g., six weeks). Thus, unless you have the ready cash to pay off your loan balance, the offset will be made even if you have chosen to leave funds on deposit with the 401(k) plan.

Planning Alert Generally, you may not take distributions from your 401(k) plan prior to attaining age 59½. However, "hardship distributions" are allowed if they are necessary to meet an "immediate and heavy financial need." Types of expenses that satisfy the requirement of "immediate and heavy financial need" include: (1) medical expenses for you, your spouse and dependents; (2) expenses to purchase your principal residence (mortgage payments are not included); (3) payment of tuition for post-secondary education for you, your spouse, children or dependents; and (4) expenses to hold off eviction or foreclosure on your principal residence. Although hardship distributions are permissible, they are subject to a 10% early withdrawal penalty. Thus, if you are thinking about taking a hardship distribution from your 401(k) plan in order to finance the purchase of your home, you should first investigate whether your plan authorizes loans. Loans from 401(k) plans must be repaid to the plan, but are not subject to the 10% penalty. If you take a hardship withdrawal, you may not make any contributions to the plan for the next six months.

Deemed IRAs

Your employer's retirement plan may have a separate account or annuity for voluntary employee contributions. If the account or annuity meets all the applicable requirements, it is treated as an IRA, a "deemed IRA." A deemed IRA can be either a traditional IRA or a Roth IRA. The purpose behind these "deemed IRAs" is that Congress thought more individuals would open IRAs if they could open accounts through their employers. Your total contributions to a deemed IRA and an IRA you open through a bank or other sponsor may not exceed the yearly maximum (e.g., $4,000 for 2005).

Inherited Retirement Accounts

Although not part of the traditional retirement planning process, you should be aware of your options if you inherit funds as the beneficiary named in a retirement plan (e.g., traditional IRA, Roth IRA, or 401(k) plan.)

If you are the spouse of the deceased, you are generally allowed to rollover the funds into your own traditional IRA. Also, you are generally allowed to rollover the inherited retirement funds into a qualified plan maintained by your employer. For example, if you inherit funds from a traditional IRA of your deceased spouse, you may rollover the funds into a traditional IRA or 401(k) plan sponsored by your employer.

However, if you are a beneficiary of a deceased individual, other than your spouse, you do not have the option to rollover the funds into your own retirement account.

Planning Alert As a non-spouse beneficiary, you may want to withdraw all the funds from the inherited account as soon as you are able. However, unless you really need the money, you should withdraw the funds over as long a period of time as possible in order to minimize your yearly income tax liability and to maintain the tax-deferred growth within the account. The rules governing the amount of time over which you may withdraw funds are exceedingly complex and depend upon such factors as the number of other beneficiaries and their ages. You should seek the help of a professional who can advise you of your legal obligations as well as the withdrawal options that you may have available.

Social Security Benefits

As part of your retirement planning process you can't ignore the benefits that you may receive from Social Security. For many individuals, these benefits may well be their main source of retirement income. However, even if you have substantial retirement income from other sources, your Social Security benefits will generally be large enough so that you should factor them into the equation when determining your tax and financial planning goals.

The table below shows how the full retirement age (i.e., the age at which an individual is entitled to unreduced benefits) is being gradually increased.

There has been some support given to the idea of accelerating the effective dates at which a higher retirement age is required in order for an individual to receive full Social Security benefits. In addition, it is possible that the whole Social Security system will be substantially revamped within the next few years.

Date of Birth*	Full benefit at age
1/1/38 or earlier	65
1938	65 + 2 months
1939	65 + 4 months
1940	65 + 6 months
1941	65 + 8 months
1942	65 + 10 months
1943-1954	66
1955	66 + 2 months

1956 .... 66 + 4 months

1957 .... 66 + 6 months

1958 .... 66 + 8 months

1959 .... 66 + 10 months

1960 or later 67

* Month and date are January 2 unless otherwise shown.

Estimation of Benefits

If you are interested in receiving an estimate of your future Social Security benefits and/or making sure that your earnings have been properly credited for Social Security purposes, and you do not automatically receive this information from the Social Security Administration (SSA), you should complete and file a Form SSA-7004 (Personal Earnings and Benefits Estimate Statement). You may obtain a copy of this form at a local Social Security office or by calling 1-800-772-1213 (or if you are hearing impaired and have access to TTY equipment, the number is 1-800-325-0778). The Social Security Administration may also be contacted on the web at http://www.ssa.gov. Form SSA-7004 may be obtained in PDF format on the web at http://www.socialsecurity.gov/online/ssa-7004.html.

Early Retirement and Post-Retirement Strategies

After a long and productive career, retirement is the goal for many for us. The result of years of successful retirement planning should be the opportunity to retire comfortably when the time is right. All of the hard work and sacrifice that went into establishing your retirement nest egg can be lost if proper planning for early retirement and/or post-retirement is neglected.

Planning for Early Retirement

Several financial considerations are brought to bear on the decision to take early retirement. One factor may be the early retirement package offered from an employer. Other sources of retirement income, such as pension plans, annuities and investments, must be assessed to determine whether the projected income will meet your retirement needs, goals and objectives. Your planning process should also include an analysis of the income tax consequences of each potential factor when making your decision.

The most telling analysis will be when you "do the math." There are several factors that contribute to your anticipated early retirement after-tax income that should be evaluated. Some of these include Social Security benefits, retirement accounts, and any additional tax liabilities that might arise. The following example outlines a typical assessment.

Example: James Smith, age 62, is unmarried and lives in a state that does not impose state or local income tax. His current annual salary is $79,800. His taxable income for 2005 is $71,600 ($79,800 minus the $5,000 standard deduction and the $3,200 personal exemption), resulting in a tax liability of $14,565. If he retires early, he will receive a lump-sum payment of $10,000 and a pension benefit of 30% of his average earnings for the last three years. Assume James' average earnings were $70,000, so his annual pension would be $21,000. Social Security benefits paid at age 62 would be approximately $10,000. He also has a

401(k) plan from which he could withdraw $2,000 annually and a traditional individual retirement account (IRA) from which he could take $10,000 annually. Thus, assuming retirement, his gross income would be $53,000. From this, James would subtract the $5,000 standard deduction and the $3,200 personal exemption, as well as $1,500 of non-taxable Social Security income, for total taxable income of $43,300, resulting in a tax liability of $7,490.

James' employer does not provide any retirement medical coverage. Under COBRA he can continue in the group plan by paying for the coverage in the amount of $400 per month ($4,800 annually). However, after 18 months, he will have to find outside coverage, probably at a greater cost than under COBRA. Finally, if he continues to work, he will pay FICA taxes ($6,105 based on the 2005 wage base) and commuting and other work-related expenses, estimated at 7% of his taxable income ($5,012, which is 7% of $71,600).

Income and Expenses	Working	Retired
Salary	$79,800	
Lump-sum distribution		$10,000
Social Security benefits (85% is taxable)		$10,000
Pension income		$21,000
401(k) income		$2,000
IRA income		$10,000
Federal income tax	($14,565)	($7,490)
FICA tax	($6,105)	
Commuting and work-related expenses	($5,012)	
Medical insurance premiums		($4,800)
Available income	$54,118	$40,710

Social Security Benefits

The age of retirement is a consideration. If you are under age 62 and not disabled, you cannot collect Social Security benefits. If you elect to commence benefits at age 62, then you will receive reduced benefits. As a retiree who is full retirement age or older, you can continue to work and earn an unlimited amount of income without causing a reduction in Social Security benefits. However, if you are a retiree under full retirement age, you can earn up to $12,000 in 2005 (the exemption amount) without any reduction in your benefits. See page 72 for a discussion of the "full retirement age."

Retirement Accounts

The earlier you retire, the less time there will be for you to contribute to a retirement plan. Since most benefits are tied to compensation, early retirement will preclude future promotions and salary raises that could lead to greater pension benefits. Also, if IRA and 401(k) accounts are drawn on for income as the result of early retirement, then a smaller amount is accumulated on a tax-deferred basis and the funds are depleted earlier instead of remaining untouched until normal retirement age.

 Tax Tip The potential tax advantages offered by a Roth IRA are important considerations in your decision about whether to transfer all or a portion of your retirement funds to this retirement funding option. See page 66.

Medical Benefits

While you are still working, your employer may pay the cost of your medical coverage wholly or at least in part. If you are age 65 or older, you can apply for Medicare. If you are under age 65, take early retirement and begin to collect Social Security benefits, you are not eligible for Medicare. However, you can obtain medical coverage through COBRA at your own expense.

Estimated Tax Liability

In order to avoid any penalty for underpayment of estimated tax, you must consider the impact of one-time payments on tax liability in the year of retirement. One-time payments can include severance payments or retirement benefits paid in a lump-sum and not rolled over into a traditional IRA. To determine whether any estimated tax penalties apply, withholding is treated as having been made in the amount of 25% of your estimated tax liability in each of the quarterly tax periods even if actually withheld later in the year. Also, you can rely on the safe harbor provision and pay 100% of your prior year's tax liability to avoid any penalty. However, if you are a high-income taxpayer in 2005 (a taxpayer with adjusted gross income of over $75,000, or $150,000 on a joint return), your safe harbor percentage is 110%. See page 106.

 Tax Tip There is an exception from the estimated tax rules for some newly retired retirees. If you retire after age 62, you can apply for relief from underpayment penalties if the underpayment results from reasonable cause and not due to willful neglect. This relief is available only in the year of retirement or in the preceding tax year.

Liquidation of Assets

If you take early retirement, you may consider converting nonproductive assets to productive investments to provide sufficient cash flow to meet your income needs. Generally, the most valuable and unproductive asset that people have is their personal residence. There are several methods for producing income from this asset. You can sell your home, and rent or purchase a less expensive home. If you are married you will probably be able to exclude up to $500,000 of gain. The exclusion is $250,000 for other taxpayers. As an alternative, you can remain in your home and obtain a reverse mortgage that will provide a monthly payment to you based on the amount of your equity.

Planning Alert If you decide to accept an early retirement package from your employer, this may translate to a fixed income. Unless you seek other employment or start your own business, your income will become virtually frozen. Accordingly, make a realistic determination of the adequacy of your anticipated retirement income to meet your future needs taking into account inflation.

Loan Qualification

If you intend to apply for a loan, such as a home equity loan or automobile loan, you may want to complete the loan application process before accepting early retirement. It may be easier to qualify for such a loan while you are still employed.

Post-Retirement Planning

Once you retire, there are several aspects of your financial picture that will require modification and adjustment to meet your changing needs. Those areas include asset management and protection, long-term health care and medical coverage, and planning for incapacity and housing in your retirement years.

Asset Protection

After retirement, planning remains important because you are no longer creating wealth and your assets may be subject to the risk of being depleted or eroded.

Insurance. One asset protection strategy is to have adequate liability insurance coverage. Homeowner and automobile insurance policies should be evaluated for adequate liability coverage for losses from accidents, thefts, disasters and personal injury claims. An umbrella liability policy may be purchased to fill in any gaps in coverage. Also, depending on the nature of your business or profession, commercial or professional liability insurance should be considered.

Tax Tip Umbrella liability insurance is designed to supplement the liability coverage provided by homeowners and automobile insurance policies. When purchasing an umbrella liability policy, it is recommended that the policy limits should be at least equal to your net worth to provide adequate protection.

Transfers between family members. Intrafamily transfers and gifts of assets can protect your property from creditors. However, the loss of control and beneficial enjoyment of the transferred assets can be a disadvantage to this method. Also, federal gift tax may be incurred if the gift is to someone other than your spouse. An alternative to an outright transfer of property to a family member is a transfer of property to a trust. Trusts provide asset protection and generally have a determinable termination date.

Business entities. If you still are engaged in an active business after retirement, the form of your business entity should be reviewed toward limiting your exposure to future liability. There are five types of business entities that provide varying degrees of asset protection and they are discussed on page 109.

Title to property. Another method of protecting assets from creditor claims is to retitle your property. Assets can be transferred between family members or converted to exempt status, such as participation in a defined benefit plan.

Planning Alert Any transfer of assets between older family members should be coordinated with existing estate plans, both yours and theirs, to maximize use and control of the assets.

Joint ownership. Joint tenancy with the right of survivorship is a form of property ownership between two or more persons in which each joint tenant has an equal right to the property during their lifetime. Joint tenants have a right of survivorship that results in the property being automatically transferred to the remaining joint tenants upon the death of a joint tenant. Assets held in joint tenancy are subject to risk since creditors of any joint tenant can attach the property.

Tenancy by the entirety is a form of property ownership between husband and wife. Each spouse has an equal, undivided interest in the property and neither spouse can sell or encumber the property without the consent of the other spouse. Thus, only creditors of both spouses jointly can attach tenancy by the entirety property.

Powers of attorney. A power of attorney is written authorization that designates someone to act on behalf of another. It may grant broad authority to make decisions concerning all financial transactions or may limit authority to one or more specific matters. Generally, a power of attorney is effective upon execution and terminates when the principal granting the power becomes incompetent. However, a durable power of attorney can be created when it includes required language that the document is to remain in effect despite the principal's incapacity or disability. The execution of a durable power of attorney ensures that your assets will be managed and financial matters will be handled in the event of permanent disability.

Living trusts. A living trust is a revocable trust set up during one's lifetime. In addition to being a way to avoid probate, a living trust provides a method for the centralized management of all assets in the trust. Typically, a living trust designates a family member or third party to act as trustee in the event that the grantor becomes incapacitated.

Asset Management and Allocation

Asset management and allocation can generate more current income. Generally, you should use personal savings, such as certificates of deposits and bonds, as sources of income first since the use of those funds will trigger few if any income tax consequences. Withdrawals from qualified retirement plans and traditional IRAs should be postponed as long as possible because these sources of income produce tax results that could erode retirement savings. The longer such funds remain tax-deferred, the larger your income buildup will be.

Reducing or eliminating debt repayment from your monthly budget is another way to increase your cash flow. As you near retirement, it is advisable to consolidate loans and pay them off as soon as possible. Other examples of how to cut back on expenses and maximize your retirement dollars include keeping your automobile for a longer period of time and utilizing discounts for seniors.

Long-Term Health Care

Rising medical costs, chronic illnesses and catastrophic illnesses can produce health care issues that need to be addressed in post-retirement planning. The principal source of health coverage for many older Americans is Medicare, the federal health insurance program financed through FICA and self-employment tax. Although the program is designed to provide basic health coverage, there are a number of gaps in coverage resulting from copayments and deductibles. Also, Medicare does not provide for long-term medical care except in certain limited circumstances.

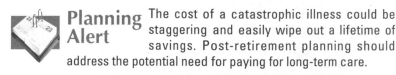 **Planning Alert** The cost of a catastrophic illness could be staggering and easily wipe out a lifetime of savings. Post-retirement planning should address the potential need for paying for long-term care.

You can obtain long-term health care insurance to pay for all or a portion of the cost of long-term care if needed. In addition to comparing the cost of such policies, other factors to consider when purchasing long-term health care insurance include: (1) the amount of daily benefit paid; (2) home care coverage; (3) the benefit period; (4) the elimination period; and (5) the benefit trigger. You may be able to deduct the premium payments as an itemized medical deduction. See page 33.

If you are self-employed or work for a small employer (with 50 or fewer employees), you can contribute to an Archer medical savings account (Archer MSA). You can establish an Archer MSA if you have no other health plan (except a high-deductible health plan) and your contributions will be tax deductible in computing adjusted gross income. Under current law, an Archer MSA cannot be established after December 31, 2005. This date may be legislatively extended. Other health accounts, such as Health Savings Accounts (HSAs), are also available. See page 118.

Incapacity

The consequences of becoming mentally incapacitated are substantial because someone who is incapacitated can no longer take any legal actions such as transferring property, writing checks, or borrowing money. There are various planning techniques that may be used to avoid the difficulties caused by incapacity.

Durable power of attorney. A durable power of attorney allows a trusted family member, friend, or professional to deal with one's financial matters during incapacity.

Power of attorney for health care. This directive specifies in advance the type and extent of medical treatment you wish to receive or not to receive and designates someone to make medical decisions on your behalf. Other types of medical directives include living wills, health care proxies and do-not-resuscitate orders.

Revocable trusts. A revocable trust is a trust that is created during one's lifetime. It can be amended or revoked at anytime but becomes irrevocable at death or incapacity. The grantor appoints a trustee to manage the assets of the trust in the event of death or incapacity. Although no income tax savings are generated when the trust is created, assets transferred to the trust will avoid probate.

Disability income insurance. A prolonged period of disability can have a substantial financial impact resulting from the loss of income and increased medical expenses. When purchasing a disability income insurance policy, the benefits should be sufficient to replace a portion of the income you earned before the disability occurred.

Housing

The choice of where to live after retirement is a major decision. Although many individuals stay in their homes, some decide to downsize to a smaller home, rent, relocate to an adult community or housing facility, or move to another state. Factors in this decision may include financial concerns, accessibility, convenience and personal security.

Remaining at home. Your personal residence often represents one of your major financial assets. Although your home may be paid off by retirement, you may not have sufficient income to keep up with its required maintenance or improvements. Or you may choose to move to another location for a variety of reasons such as health concerns or to be closer to relatives. The availability of community support services should be considered when evaluating whether to continue living in your home or choose another option.

Assisted living facilities. Assisted living residences are designed for those who need some assistance in the activities of daily life but not necessarily medical supervision. Such facilities may be part of a retirement community, nursing home or adult housing, and generally include group meals, emergency call systems, housekeeping, laundry, transportation and recreational activities. Some assisted living facilities offer nursing home levels of long-term personal care and provide dedicated Alzheimer units in relatively pleasant surroundings at prices competitive with more traditional nursing home facilities. Entrance fees and ongoing monthly expenses should be weighed when considering these housing options.

Long-term care facilities. A nursing home is a residence that provides a room, meals, recreation, assistance with daily activities and a level of nursing services to its residents. Factors to consider when choosing a nursing home include: (1) religious and cultural preferences; (2) Medicare and Medicaid participation; (3) availability; (4) special care needs; and (5) location. There are also different levels of nursing home care depending on your personal health care needs.

Medicaid planning. For most families, the thought of transferring assets to qualify for Medicaid occurs too late to take advantage of a number of ways of doing so. Planning professionals can provide help to those who think ahead and recognize this potential problem.

Estate Planning—Minimizing Estate and Gift Taxes

Your tax planning is not complete without a review of your estate plan. If your estate is large enough to potentially be subject to estate tax you can take steps now to minimize that liability and to ensure that the greatest possible share of your estate goes to your heirs rather than to the government.

You have undoubtedly heard that the estate tax was repealed through tax legislation enacted in 2001. The repeal, however, is phased in over a nine-year period that began in 2002. The repeal will be fully effective for decedents dying in 2010. Due to a sunset provision in the 2001 Act, the estate tax will be *fully* reinstated in 2011, unless Congress acts to make the repeal permanent.

Gift tax planning issues go hand in hand with the estate tax. So it is important to know that the law also reduces the gift tax rate over the same nine-year phase-in period. However, the gift tax will not be eliminated and will remain in force after 2009. In addition, estate and gift taxes are no longer "unified" in that, since 2004, the exclusion amounts for each are different.

Why does the law reinstate the estate tax after ten years? Basically, the repeal period had to be limited in order to sidestep a complex procedural rule that opponents could have used to stop the legislation from moving forward.

Will the repeal be extended? The answer will depend on political and economic factors that can't be foreseen now. This uncertainty, in conjunction with the phase-in of the estate and gift tax rate reductions, makes it important to work closely with your professional advisor to tailor and refine, as necessary, your estate plan to take full advantage of the changing estate tax landscape.

Estate Tax Exclusion

Every estate is entitled to an exclusion that effectively protects a certain amount of property from the estate tax. As a result of the 2001 legislation, the amount of the exclusion will increase annually up to $3.5 million by 2009. There will be no exclusion in 2010 because the estate tax is completely repealed in that year. In 2011, the exclusion will drop back to $1 million unless Congress extends the repeal of the estate tax.

The following chart compares the exclusion amounts under both the old law and the new law:

Year of death:	Old exclusion amount:	New exclusion amount:
2005	$950,000	$1,500,000
2006 through 2008	$1,000,000	$2,000,000
2009	$1,000,000	$3,500,000
2010	$1,000,000	N/A
2011 and thereafter	$1,000,000	$1,000,000

Marital Deduction

For many estates, the marital deduction is the most valuable statutory element available. The marital deduction is an unlimited deduction for property that passes to your surviving spouse.

 Planning Alert Many wills include standard language that provides that beneficiaries other than the surviving spouse will receive an amount equal to the available estate tax exclusion. The remaining portion of the estate is given to the surviving spouse and escapes the estate tax by virtue of the marital deduction. In this way, the estate tax is entirely avoided at the death of the first spouse. A provision in a will which contains such an automatic allocation, however, may need to be reviewed in light of the significant increase in the estate tax exclusion ($1.5 million in 2005 to $3.5 million in 2009). An automatic provision could give heirs other than your spouse more than you intended to and, depending upon the size of your estate, unwittingly cut your spouse out altogether.

Lifetime Gift Tax Exclusion

The gift tax affects the amount of gifts that you may make during your life. As explained below, you may give up to $11,000 to each donee in 2005 without paying any gift tax. You are also entitled to a lifetime gift tax exclusion for gifts that are not covered by the annual exclusion. In

2005, the lifetime exclusion is set at $1 million, at which point it holds steady and diverges from the rising estate tax exclusion. The gift tax exclusion will remain at $1 million after 2010, when the estate tax will be reinstated.

The amount of the estate tax exclusion (discussed above) is effectively reduced by the portion of the gift tax exclusion that you use during your lifetime. For example, if you die in 2005 and you previously took full advantage of the $1 million gift tax exclusion, only $500,000 of the otherwise $1.5 million estate tax exclusion is available.

 Tax Tip Instead of leaving everything to one's spouse, the use of a marital deduction trust and a nonmarital trust will often maximize estate tax savings. The nonmarital trust provides the surviving spouse with needed income during life. Yet, because the survivor lacks control over the trust, the assets are not included in his or her estate upon death. On the other hand, the marital deduction trust provides the survivor with the bulk of the funds needed during life. If planned correctly, the two trusts will help ensure that the liability for estate taxes is minimized.

Make Use of the Annual Gift Tax Exclusion

If you have substantial assets, you can make a significant reduction in your taxable estate by making gifts that are shielded from gift tax by the annual gift tax exclusion. The annual gift tax exclusion protects the first $11,000 of gifts you make to each donee in 2005. The exclusion cannot be carried over to future years, so you must make your transfers by December 31, 2005, in order to make use of the 2005 exclusion. If your spouse lacks separate resources to take advantage of the exclusion, you can give $22,000 to each donee provided your spouse consents to the gift splitting. For example, using gift splitting, a couple with five children could give each child $22,000 for a total of $110,000 in annual exclusion gifts in one year. The annual gift tax exclusion will be adjusted for inflation in future years.

Educational or Medical Expense Exclusion

If you are interested in making gifts in order to avoid or limit any future estate tax and you have reached the maximum annual amount on your tax-free gifts, you should be aware of the fact that gifts used for tuition or medical expenses are not subject to the year 2005 $11,000 maximum annual exclusion.

An unlimited gift tax exclusion is allowed for amounts paid on behalf of a donee directly to an educational organization, provided such amounts constitute tuition payments. For example, amounts that you pay for books, dormitory fees, or board on behalf of the donee are not eligible for the exclusion.

Amounts paid directly to health care providers for medical services on behalf of a donee also qualify for the unlimited exclusion gift tax exclusion.

These exclusions from the gift tax are available without regard to the relationship between you and the donee.

Gift and Estate Tax Rates

The gift and estate tax rates are identical until 2010 when the estate tax is repealed. In 2010, the maximum gift tax rate will be 35 percent, which under other provisions of the 2001 Act is also the highest income tax rate for individuals.

The gift and estate tax rates range from 18 percent to 47 percent in 2005. The top rate decreases over time and reaches 45 percent in 2007. The lower rate brackets remain in place until 2010, when the estate tax is completely repealed. However, keep in mind that the estate and gift tax exclusion amounts are increased during the phase-out period which ends in 2010. This will reduce estate and gift taxes for estates that are not large enough to receive the additional benefit of the reduction in the top rate during the phaseout period and it will also serve to completely eliminate many smaller estates from the payment of estate taxes.

Year	Top Estate and Gift Tax Rate
2005	47%
2006	46%
2007-2009	45%
2010	35% (gift tax only)

After 2010, unless Congress extends the estate tax repeal, the former rate schedule from 2000, with the top 55-percent tax bracket, will be reinstated.

Stepped-Up Basis Rule

When your heirs receive property, their basis is generally stepped-up to the fair market value of the property at the date of your death. This stepped-up basis rule is extremely beneficial because the recipient can avoid paying tax on the appreciation.

 Example Your estate includes stock for which you paid $1,000,000 and this stock has a fair market value of $6,000,000 when you die. Under the current rules, the person who receives the stock would take a $6,000,000 basis and could sell it immediately thereafter without recognizing a gain. Any subsequent sale would only have to take into account any increase in value above the $6,000,000 amount.

Beginning in 2010 (the year of the estate tax repeal), the law will limit the amount of property that can receive a stepped-up basis. This is one way that Congress hopes to make up for some of the lost estate tax revenue. Under this rule, an estate may only increase the basis of assets by $1.3 million. Thus, in the previous example, the stock basis could only be increased to $2.3 million if it passed through your estate in 2010.

A surviving spouse who receives assets from your estate is entitled to an additional $3 million basis step-up. Looking at the preceding example again, if the stock passes to your spouse, the basis can be increased to $5.3 million.

Assuming Congress does not extend the estate tax repeal, the old stepped-up basis rules will be reinstated beginning in 2011.

In anticipation of this change, your will or related trust instrument should explain how you want the limited step-up allocated among your appreciated assets. This should minimize any disputes on this point among beneficiaries. It is also important to start keeping records that accurately track the basis of your assets so that the appropriate basis can be determined.

Planning Alert

When you make a gift of appreciated property, the donee takes a carryover basis, which is another way of saying that the donee takes your basis at the time of the gift. The donee uses this carryover basis to determine gain or loss when the property is sold. Generally, as long as the stepped-up basis rule remains in force and you have a choice, it is ordinarily better to let highly appreciated property pass through your estate so that your heirs can take advantage of the stepped-up basis.

Planning Alert

If you have investment property that has depreciated and want to make a gift, you will generally be better off selling it first. This is because if you gift property that has declined in value, the donee takes a carryover basis to determine gain and a fair market value (fmv) basis (fmv on the date of the gift) to determine loss. Keep in mind, however, that loss can only be recognized for tax purposes when investment or business property is sold.

Example

You purchased stock for $10,000 and its current value is $4,000. If you sell the stock and give the cash as a gift you may claim a $6,000 loss ($10,000 current value - $4,000 purchase price). If you gift the stock and the donee sells it, the donee has no loss. The fair market value of the stock and the donee's basis for purposes of determining loss are the same (i.e., $4,000).

State Death Taxes

Prior to 2005, your estate could claim a federal credit for the estate or other death tax imposed by the state in which you live. The credit was limited to a maximum amount that was based on the size of your estate.

Starting in 2005, the credit for state death taxes is repealed and your estate is instead able to *deduct* state death taxes that it pays. While the credit was of equal value to all estates (a credit reduces an estate's tax liability dollar for dollar), the deduction favors larger estates that would otherwise be in the highest estate tax brackets.

The repeal of the credit may reduce the amount of your state estate tax liability, but it will not necessarily reduce the estate's total transfer tax liability. Most states currently impose an estate tax that is equal to the maximum state tax credit that can be claimed by your estate for federal purposes. This is usually done through a "pick-up" or "soak-up" tax that ensures that the final state death tax bill is at least equal to the maximum state tax credit allowed under federal law. If you live in a state with a pure "pick-up" or "soak-up" tax, your state estate liability tax should decrease as a result of this change. Keep in mind that some states have rewritten their estate tax laws to recoup the amount of estate tax that they will lose as a result of the reduction and repeal of the federal state death tax credit. In addition, some states peg their tax to the federal credit as of a certain date before passage of the 2001 Act. Consequently, in those states a decedent's estate may actually end up paying more in total transfer taxes than before the 2001 Act was enacted.

Generation-Skipping Transfer Tax

The generation-skipping transfer (GST) tax is a tax on the transfer of property to a person who is more than one generation younger than you (for example, your grandchild). The GST is on the same schedule for reduction and repeal as the estate tax. In addition, individuals are currently allowed an exemption from the GST tax in an amount that is the same as the applicable estate tax exclusion ($1.5 million in 2005).

Family Strategies

Chances are that you are in a higher tax bracket than your children. If so, you may be able to save taxes by shifting income to children or other family members in lower brackets even if they are under age 14 and subject to the "kiddie tax."

Shifting Income to Your Kids

The strategy of putting investment property in your kids' names to take advantage of their lower tax rates still lives, even after the advent of the kiddie tax, for two reasons:

(1) The kiddie tax does not apply to kids who are 14 and over by the end of the year. The rules that tax your children's investment income at your tax rate do not apply once the children reach the age of 14. Chances are that at that age your children are still in a low tax bracket and tax savings can be a help in sending them off to college.

(2) Current transfers pay off in later years. A program of annual gifts to your children of up to $11,000 per child for 2005 ($22,000 if you are married) can transfer a sizable portion of your estate to your children without gift or estate tax liability and, at the same time, increase the amount of income that will be taxed at your children's rates once they reach the age of 14.

An alternative available to you if you run your own business is to hire your kids to work for you. Earned income is not subject to the kiddie tax, so this technique allows you to shift funds to your lower-bracket family members and to get work done in the process. As an added bonus, you may be able to deduct the payments as a business expense, as long as they are reasonable compensation for services that the child actually performed. If your child is under 14 you can also avoid the kiddie tax by transferring or investing in assets that appreciate and do not generate any taxable income until they are sold, such as non-dividend paying stock or land.

Planning for the kiddie tax. The kiddie tax separates and taxes a child's unearned income (dividends, interest, gains from the sale or exchange of property) in three distinct ways:

(1) unearned income up to $800 in 2005 is not taxed;

(2) unearned income between $801 and $1,600 in 2005 is taxed at 10 percent; and

(3) unearned income over $1,600 is taxed at the parents' rate.

The shifting of assets to a child can result in substantial tax savings. For example, a transfer of assets to a child that produces $1,600 in income to the child would save a 35%-bracket family $480 (35% of $1,600 minus 10% of $800). A family in the 33% bracket would save $448, while a family in the 28% bracket would save $368.

Parents may be able to elect to include unearned income subject to the kiddie tax directly on their return. To make this election, the child's income must consist solely of dividends, interest, or capital gain distributions that amount to more than $800 but no more than $8,000 in 2005. The income in excess of $1,600 is taxed at the parents' highest bracket rate. No tax is imposed on the first $800 of income and income between $800 and $1,600 is taxed at a 10-percent rate.

If this election is made, the additional income increases the parents' AGI, which, in turn, could cost the family deductions and credits that are tied to AGI, such as medical expenses and miscellaneous itemized deductions (see Appendix F). The additional income will also probably increase state and local income tax liabilities. A bigger AGI, however, could allow you to claim larger charitable contribution deductions. Also, the inclusion of your child's investment income on your return could increase your allowable deduction for investment interest since that deduction is limited to investment income.

 Tax Tip If you make the election, you must attach a Form 8814, "Parents' Election to Report Child's Interest and Dividends," to your own tax return. If you do not make the election, a Form 8615, "Tax for Children Under Age 14 With Investment Income of More than $1,600," generally must be attached to the tax return filed by or on behalf of the child.

Protecting Dependency Exemptions

If you expect to claim a dependency exemption for someone other than a qualifying child, you will lose the exemption if that person has gross income in excess of $3,200. In that case, you should consider curtailing or deferring the dependent's excess income for the rest of the year if the lost or deferred income is more than made up by the tax savings produced by the exemption. Switching to tax-exempt municipal bonds or to U.S. savings bonds can reduce income from investments that give rise to taxable income. (However, you might realize a capital gain on the transactions.)

Legislation Highlight Beginning in 2005, under the Working Families Tax Relief Act of 2004 (P.L. 108-311), a uniform definition of a child applies and the definition of a dependent has been rewritten to categorize each dependent as a "qualifying child" or a "qualifying relative." Under the new uniform definition, a taxpayer's children include the taxpayer's natural children, stepchildren, adopted children and eligible foster children. (The new uniform definition also applies for purposes of the child tax credit, the earned income tax credit, the child and dependent care credit, and head-of-household filing status.)

To be a "qualifying child" for purposes of the dependency exemption, an individual:

- must be under the age of 19 at the end of the year or be a full-time student under the age of 24;
- must share a home with the taxpayer for more than half the year;
- must not provide more than half of his or her own support;
- must be the taxpayer's child, or a descendent of the taxpayer's child (the taxpayer's grandchild); or be the taxpayer's brother or sister, or a descendent of the taxpayer's brother or sister (the taxpayer's niece or nephew, related by blood).

The exemption tests for a "qualifying relative" are basically the same as the pre-2005 tests for all dependents. Thus, a qualifying relative:

- must receive at least one-half of total annual support from the taxpayer;
- must not have gross income in excess of the annual exemption amount ($3,200 in 2005);
- must either be related to the taxpayer, or share the taxpayer's home and be a member of the taxpayer's household.

As under prior law, both qualifying children and qualifying relatives generally must be U.S. citizens or nationals; or residents of the U.S., Canada or Mexico. This test does not apply to a taxpayer's legally adopted child who shares the taxpayer's home as a member of the taxpayer's household. Also, as under prior law, a married dependent must not file a joint return.

The deduction for personal and dependency exemptions is phased out as adjusted gross income exceeds threshold amounts that are indexed for inflation. For 2005, the adjusted gross income thresholds that trigger the beginning of the phaseout are as follows:

2005
Phaseout of Exemptions

Filing Status	AGI Threshold Phaseout Amount	Complete AGI Phaseout Amount After
Married Filing Separately	$109,475	$170,725
Single	$145,950	$268,450
Head of Household	$182,450	$304,950
Married Filing Jointly	$218,950	$341,450
Qualifying Widow(er)	$218,950	$341,450

Beginning in 2006, the dependency exemption phaseout will be repealed over a five-year period.

Multiple Support Agreements

In order to claim a dependency exemption for another person, you must usually provide more than one-half of that person's support. However, there may be situations in which you and others are paying at least half of the support of another person (such as an elderly parent) but no one is individually paying more than 50 percent of the total support. In this situation, you can generally agree among yourselves who is entitled to the dependency exemption. The person claiming the exemption must provide at least 10 percent of the dependent's total support. Everyone who provides at least 10 percent of the total support (and could claim the exemption but for the 50-percent support test) must complete Form 2120, "Multiple Support Declaration." The person who claims the exemption must attach these completed forms to his or her return.

 Planning Alert In a multiple support situation, you may want to rotate the exemption from year to year among the group that is providing the dependent's support. The group may also consider giving the exemption to the group member in the highest tax bracket.

 Tax Tip Keep in mind that certain relatives may qualify as dependents even though they do not live with you (e.g., children, parents, aunts and uncles). The gross income of a person claimed as a dependent, however, cannot exceed $3,200 in 2005. Gross income does not include nontaxable income such as Social Security benefits.

Dependency Exemptions of Divorced Parents

If you are a divorced parent, your entitlement to dependency exemptions for your children does not depend on the amount of contributions that you and your former spouse each make to the children's support (although your combined contributions must meet the general support requirement applicable to all dependents). The general rule is that, as long as at least half of a child's support is provided by one or both parents, the parent who has custody of a child is entitled to a deduction unless he or she relinquishes it to the other parent or unless the parents' divorce decree or separation agreement provides that the noncustodial parent is entitled to the deduction. If you are a divorced parent, your year-end tax planning should include a consideration of which parent would most benefit by the dependency exemption and the effect this may have on the amount of child support to be paid.

 **Planning Alert** You should also keep in mind that the child tax credit is tied to the dependency exemption. You cannot claim the credit for a child unless you are also entitled to claim that child as a dependent.

Adoption Expenses

Individuals may claim a tax credit of up to $10,630 in 2005 for qualified adoption expenses, such as legal fees and court costs. The amount of the credit is not affected by your marital status and applies to each adoption. If you adopt a special needs child you may claim a $10,630 credit even if your actual expenses are less than $10,630. The credit is phased-out ratably at modified adjusted gross income levels between $159,450 and $199,450.

You may claim the adoption credit against your regular and alternative minimum tax liability. Although your credit may not reduce your regular and AMT liability below zero, you can carry forward any unused credit for up to five years.

Expenses paid or incurred before the year that an adoption is finalized are taken into account in computing the credit in the following year. Expenses paid or incurred during or after the year an adoption is finalized are taken into account in the year that the expense is paid or incurred. However, no credit for a special needs adoption may be claimed until the year that the adoption is finalized.

In addition to the adoption credit, the law allows an employee to exclude up to $10,630 for amounts received under an employer's adoption assistance program. The adoption credit may not be claimed for excluded amounts that are used to pay adoption expenses. If you adopt a special needs child, the $10,630 exclusion applies regardless of the amount spent on the adoption.

Child Tax Credit

Taxpayers who have qualifying children under the age of 17 are entitled to a $1,000 per child tax credit in 2005. The credit begins to phase out when modified adjusted gross income reaches $110,000 for joint filers, $55,000 for married taxpayers filing separately, and $75,000 for singles. The credit is reduced by $50 for each $1,000 of modified AGI above the thresholds.

 Planning Alert The credit is $1,000 through 2010. It is scheduled to revert to $500 for 2011 and later years under a "sunset" rule. You can claim the child tax credit against your regular and AMT tax liability. In 2005, the credit is "refundable" (that is, payable even if you don't have a tax liability) to the extent of 15 percent of your earned income in excess of $11,000.

The Marriage Penalty

Married couples filing their first joint return often discover one downside to married life—the so-called "marriage penalty." Due to the differential in the standard deduction amount and the structure of the tax brackets, married couples may owe more taxes filing jointly than they would pay if they had remained single and filed their own returns.

The marriage penalty does not hit every married couple. It usually only affects married persons who both work. If only one spouse works, the couple will usually pay less in taxes by filing a joint return.

If you are planning your marriage, remember that your marital status is determined on the last day of the year. Putting the element of romance aside, if you are considering a late 2005 wedding, it may pay you to wait until early 2006 to tie the knot and reduce your 2005 tax bill.

 Planning Alert Congress has taken steps to eliminate many aspects of the marriage penalty. In 2005 through 2010, the standard deduction for married persons is 200 percent (twice) the amount of the standard deduction for single filers.

In addition, the amount of taxable income that falls into the 10-or 15-percent tax brackets for joint filers is also twice the amount of a single taxpayer's taxable income that is subject to those rates. This change only lessens the marriage penalty in the 10-or 15-percent brackets. Single filers still have an advantage in the remaining tax brackets (the 25-, 28-, 33-, and 35-percent brackets).

Child and Dependent Care Credit

If you reside in a household that includes a dependent child under the age of 13 or a dependent or spouse who is mentally or physically incapable of caring for himself, you can claim a credit for expenses paid to provide for the dependent's care. The key condition is that those expenses must enable you to be employed or to look for work. The maximum amount of expenses for which a credit may be claimed is $3,000 if one person is cared for and $6,000 if care is provided for two or more people, but any employer-provided dependent care assistance (including your contributions to a dependent care FSA account) reduces the maximum amount on a dollar-for-dollar basis.

The credit equals 35 percent of eligible expenses for individuals with AGI of $15,000 or less. The credit percentage decreases by one percent for each additional $2,000 of AGI, or portion thereof. The minimum credit percentage is 20 percent and applies once AGI exceeds $43,000. The amount on which the credit is computed is limited to the lower of eligible expenses or, for married couples, the earned income of the lower-paid spouse. A non-wage-earning spouse who is disabled or who is a full-time student is treated as having earned income in the amount of $250 per month if there is one person requiring care in the household, and $500 per month if there are two or more persons requiring care.

 Legislation Highlight Beginning in 2005, the Working Families Tax Relief Act of 2004 (P.L. 108-311) eliminates the requirement that a taxpayer maintain a household in order to claim the child and dependent care credit. If all other requirements are met, you may be able to claim the credit with respect to a qualifying individual who lives with you for more than one-half of the year, even if you do not provide more than one-half of the cost of maintaining the household. To be a qualifying individual for purposes of the credit, a disabled dependent or spouse of a taxpayer must have the same principal place of abode as the taxpayer for more than one-half of the tax year.

 Tax Tip Remember, if you hire someone to care for your children and the care is provided in your home, the IRS will generally consider you an employer. If you pay the domestic worker more than $1,400 during 2005, you will be liable for the employer's share of FICA tax. You need not withhold federal income tax unless the domestic worker asks you to withhold and you agree. Any tax that you owe because of your employer status, is generally reported on

Schedule H, "Household Employment Taxes," which is filed with your Form 1040.

 Planning Alert Generally, if you have a choice between claiming the child and dependent care credit or participating in a dependent care flexible spending account (FSA) (see page 22), you will save more taxes by paying your child care expenses with FSA money.

For example, you and your spouse both work, and day care for your two children in 2005 costs $10,000. Your taxable income is $80,000, which places you in the 25-percent tax bracket, and your AGI is over $43,000, which means your dependent care credit is limited to 20 percent of your qualified expenses up to $6,000. Thus, your dependent care credit for 2005 is $1,200 ($6,000 x 20%). If you contribute $5,000 to an FSA, you will save $1,250 ($5,000 x 25%) in federal income tax. Furthermore, you get an additional tax savings of $383 ($5,000 x 7.65%) because you don't have to pay the 7.65% social security tax on amounts contributed to an FSA. If you only had one child, your maximum credit would be cut in half to $600 ($3,000 x 20%). Your FSA tax savings, however, would remain unchanged assuming you spent $5,000 on day care.

Education Incentives

In the past few years Congress has provided numerous tax incentives for individuals who decide to further their education beyond high school. The most important of these incentives are the:

- Hope and lifetime learning tax credits;
- Coverdell education savings accounts;
- penalty-free withdrawals from traditional and Roth IRAs for higher education expenses;
- above-the-line deductions for higher education expenses and student loan interest;
- qualified tuition programs;
- a $5,250 exclusion for employer-provided educational assistance; and
- an exclusion for interest from educational savings bonds.

Education Tax Credits

Two tax credits may be elected by low- and middle-income individuals for qualified expenses incurred by students pursuing post-secondary education. Eligible expenses include tuition and fees but not books, room and board, insurance, transportation or student activity costs. The Hope scholarship credit provides a maximum allowable credit for 2005 of $1,500 per student for each of the first two years of post-secondary education, and the life-time learning credit allows a credit of 20 percent of qualified tuition expenses paid by the taxpayer for any year the Hope credit is not claimed. Generally, you can't claim other education incentive deductions for expenses that are taken into account in computing these credits.

Planning Alert Keep in mind that tuition paid in December 2005 for a course that begins in January 2006 is counted towards the 2005 credit, not the 2006 credit. Also, remember that you may be able to reduce the amount of your federal income tax withholding based on the estimated tax benefits of the education credits and deductions.

The Hope scholarship credit allows taxpayers a 100-percent credit per eligible student for the first $1,000 of tuition expenses and a 50-percent credit for the second $1,000 of tuition paid. The student must be enrolled on at least a half time basis for at least one academic period during the year.

The lifetime learning credit is available for up to 20 percent of qualified tuition and related expenses incurred (up to $2,000) for a qualified student pursuing post-secondary education. Qualified expenses include expenses for undergraduate or graduate-level and professional degree courses, as well as expenses for any course of instruction at an eligible educational institution to acquire or improve job skills, even if it is not part of a degree program or the student is not enrolled on at least a half-time basis.

Both credits can be claimed for the same student, but not for the same expenses. However, a taxpayer may not claim both credits for the same student for the same tax year.

Tax Tip Is a deduction or exclusion better than a tax credit? The answer depends upon your tax bracket. A deduction or exclusion reduces the amount of taxable income that falls within your tax bracket. A credit, on the other hand, reduces, dollar for dollar, the amount of tax that you compute on your taxable income. For example, suppose that you are in the 25-percent tax bracket. You have a choice between claiming a $1,000 deduction or a $200 tax credit. You should claim the deduction. By claiming the deduction you will save $250 ($1,000 x 25%) in taxes. If you claim the credit you only save $200 in taxes. On the other hand, if you are in the 15-percent tax bracket, the deduction would only save you $150 ($1,000 x 15%) in taxes and you would be better off claiming the $200 credit.

Both credits are available for qualified tuition and related expenses incurred for yourself, your spouse, or your dependents. The Hope credit maximum is allowed per student, while the lifetime learning credit maximum is calculated per taxpayer and does not vary based on the number of students in your family. Also, the lifetime learning credit is available for an unlimited number of years and is available for both undergraduate and graduate or professional degree expenses. The allowable amount of the credits is reduced for taxpayers who have modified adjusted gross incomes in 2005 of $43,000 ($87,000 for joint returns); the credits are completely phased out when modified adjusted gross income reaches $53,000 ($107,000 for joint returns). The credits may not be claimed if you are married and filing a separate return.

Only the taxpayer who claims the student as a dependent can claim an education tax credit. If you are eligible to claim the student as a dependent, but do not, only the student may claim the credit. Form 8863, "Education Credit," is used to elect to take either credit, and is attached to Form 1040, or to an amended return filed after the due date of the return, but before the expiration of the limitations period for filing a claim for credit or refund for the tax year in which the credit is claimed.

Coverdell Education Savings Accounts

You may set up an education savings account to save for the qualified education expenses of a designated beneficiary. Previously, these accounts were called "education individual retirement accounts." They are now called "Coverdell education savings accounts" in honor of Georgia's deceased Senator Paul Coverdell.

In general, a Coverdell account is not taxable. Distributions from the account are tax-free to the beneficiary provided they do not exceed the beneficiary's qualified education expenses for the year. The maximum amount that you can contribute to a Coverdell account is $2,000 per year. Contributions must end when the beneficiary reaches age 18. The age limit does not apply for a beneficiary with special needs. Your contribution for a particular year must be made by the date for filing your tax return for that year, not including extensions.

Coverdell accounts may be used to fund higher education expenses. The accounts may also be used to fund elementary and secondary education expenses (kindergarten through grade 12) whether incurred in a public, private, or religious school. Qualified education expenses include tuition, fees, books, supplies, equipment and room and board.

The amount that can be contributed to a Coverdell account is limited for higher income taxpayers. The contribution limit is phased out for joint filers with adjusted gross incomes between $190,000 and $220,000. The phaseout range for single filers is set between $95,000 and $110,000.

 **Planning Alert** If your AGI is too high to make contributions you should arrange to have a relative with lower AGI make the contributions. Alternatively, you can make a gift to the beneficiary and have the beneficiary make the contribution.

Earnings on contributions are distributed tax-free provided they are used to pay the beneficiary's qualified education expenses. If a distribution is made from a Coverdell account in 2005, the Hope and lifetime learning credits can also be claimed, provided that the credits aren't claimed with respect to the same education expenses paid with a distribution from the Coverdell account.

If the distribution from the Coverdell account exceeds the qualified education expenses, only a portion of the distribution is excludable. In addition, distributions not used for qualified education expenses are subject to a 10-percent addition to tax. Amounts remaining in an account may be rolled over into another account for the education of another beneficiary in the original beneficiary's family, or distributed to the original beneficiary, who must include the earnings component of the distribution in income and pay a 10-percent penalty.

IRA Education Expense Withdrawals

The 10-percent tax on early withdrawals from a traditional or Roth IRA does not apply to distributions from an IRA if you use the amounts to pay qualified higher education expenses for yourself, your spouse, your child or your grandchild. Qualified higher education expenses include tuition, fees, books, supplies, and equipment required for enrollment or attendance at a post secondary institution. The amount of qualified higher education expenses is reduced by the amounts of any qualified scholarship, educational assistance allowance, or other payment that is attributable to the student's enrollment and excludable from gross income.

Education Loan Interest Deduction

If you need to borrow money in order to pay for school expenses, a deduction for the loan interest will lessen the burden. An above-the-line deduction for up to $2,500 is allowed annually for interest paid on qualified education loans. This means you can claim the deduction on Form 1040 or Form 1040A, even if you do not itemize your deductions.

A qualified education loan is any debt you incur to pay the qualified higher education expenses of yourself, your spouse, or a person who was a dependent at the time that the debt was incurred. If you are claimed as a dependent on someone else's return you can't claim the deduction. Also, only the person liable for the loan can deduct the student loan interest. Furthermore, the taxpayer cannot deduct interest paid on a student loan for a dependent unless the taxpayer actually makes the payments during the tax year for which the deduction is sought and the taxpayer claims an exemption for the dependent on that year's return.

The deduction is phased out for taxpayers with modified adjusted gross income for 2005 that is between $50,000 and $65,000 ($105,000 and $135,000 for married taxpayers filing joint returns). These phaseout ranges are adjusted for inflation.

 Tax Tip If you took out a loan to pay for your child's college expenses, you are entitled to the deduction for up to $2,500 of the interest paid on the loan, provided the loan is used strictly for college expenses. However, if your child takes out the loan, only he or she is entitled to deduct the interest on the loan, even if you pay the interest. Also, keep in mind that your child will not be eligible to deduct the interest if he or she is claimed as a dependent on your return.

 Tax Tip If you expect your adjusted gross income to exceed the limits placed on a particular education tax incentive for 2005 and would otherwise qualify for the tax break, you may want to consider deferring the receipt of income to later years or accelerating above-the-line deductions into 2005.

Deduction for Higher Education Expenses

You can also claim an above-the-line deduction of up to $4,000 of qualified tuition and related expenses paid for higher education in 2005. This deduction is not available for higher education expenses paid after 2005, though Congress might decide to extend this tax break. Qualified tuition and related expenses are tuition and fees that are required for the enrollment or attendance of you, your spouse, or your dependent, at an eligible educational institution, including accredited public, nonprofit, or proprietary post-secondary institutions. You cannot claim the deduction if you are or can be claimed as a dependent on another taxpayer's return, or if you are married and file a separate return.

For 2005, if your AGI does not exceed $65,000, or $130,000 if you file a joint return, the maximum deduction increases to $4,000. If your AGI is between $65,000 and $80,000, or between $130,000 and $160,000 for joint filers, you may deduct up to $2,000. No deduction is allowed if your AGI exceeds $80,000, or $160,000 if you file a joint return.

You cannot claim the deduction if anyone claimed the Hope or lifetime learning credit for the same student. You also cannot claim the deduction for any expenses that you deduct under another provision; for instance, if you deduct education expenses as a business expense, you cannot also deduct them as a higher education expense. However, you can claim the deduction for expenses that were not taken into account in connection with excludable distributions from a qualified tuition plan, distributions from a Coverdell savings account, or interest on an education savings bond.

Tax Tip The deduction for higher education expenses may be available to taxpayers who do not qualify for the Hope and lifetime learning credits because their AGI exceeds the phase-out thresholds. In 2005, the credits are completely phased out if the taxpayer's modified AGI exceeds $53,000, or $107,000 for joint filers; but the maximum $4,000 deduction is available for taxpayers with AGI up to $65,000, or $130,000 for joint filers.

Qualified Tuition Programs

If you are going to pay some or all of your child's college expenses, you should determine if the state in which your child plans to attend school offers a qualified tuition program. This type of program is also known as a prepaid tuition program, guaranteed tuition program, Code Sec. 529 plan or 529 program. These are all programs under which a person may purchase tuition credits or make cash contributions to an account on behalf of a beneficiary for payment of qualified higher education expenses. Some plans are guaranteed. In a plan that is not guaranteed, there is a potential risk the program's trust fund will become insolvent before the funds are needed.

Tuition programs can be set up by a state for a public school. Private institutions may also set up tuition programs. However, the qualified tuition program of a private institution cannot include a savings account plan feature. A savings account plan allows you to contribute to a savings account established by the state for the benefit of the designated beneficiary. The account usually allows you to select from a number of investment options. Typically, you can use the funds to pay for out-of-state schools. Contributions may be deductible on your state tax return.

Planning Alert The Department of Education considers prepaid tuition benefits as a resource that reduces a student's financial need on a dollar-for-dollar basis. Thus, if a prepaid tuition contract pays out $8,000 in tuition benefits for the year, in the subsequent year, the student will be considered as having $8,000 less need. Consequently, when utilizing a prepaid tuition program, a student's eligibility for subsidized loans, work-study or certain grants may be significantly reduced. More information on this issue can be found at www.ed.gov and www.ifap.ed.gov.

Distributions from a qualified tuition program that are used to pay qualified higher education expenses are tax-free. This should add an important incentive for participating in a qualified tuition program; previously the person receiving the distribution was taxed on the earnings component of the distribution under rules that apply to annuity payments. Qualified educational expenses include tuition, fees, books, supplies, and equipment required for enrollment or attendance at an eligible educational institution, as well as the reasonable costs of room and board for a designated beneficiary who is at least a half-time student. Qualified expenses also include expenses of a special needs beneficiary that are necessary for that person's enrollment or attendance at an eligible educational institution.

Contributions to the program are treated like gifts. A lump-sum contribution of $55,000 can be treated as if made over a five-year period. If you make this election, you will not exceed the $11,000 per-year gift-tax exclusion.

You can exclude amounts distributed by a qualified tuition program from income and claim other educational credits, deductions or exclusions, as long as the distribution is not used for the same expenses. Thus, qualifying educational expenses taken into account for purposes of the exclusion cannot include expenses taken into account in determining the Hope or lifetime learning credits, excludable employer-provided educational assistance, or excludable scholarships. If a designated beneficiary receives distributions from both a qualified tuition program and a Coverdell education savings account that exceed the beneficiary's qualified higher education expenses, the expenses must be allocated between the distributions.

Employer's Educational Assistance Program

Your employer may have set up an educational assistance program. This type of program allows you to exclude up to $5,250 in employer provided educational assistance from your income. As an added bonus, expenses for graduate courses also qualify for the exclusion. The courses covered by an employer's educational assistance program do not have to relate to your job.

 Planning Alert If you take full advantage of your employer's educational assistance program and exclude $5,250 from your income, your tax savings will depend upon your tax bracket. For example, if you are in the 25-percent bracket (your 2005 taxable income is between

$59,400 and $119,950 if you are married and file jointly or between $29,700 and $71,950 if you are single), you will save $1,313 ($5,250 x 25%).

Exclusion for U.S. Savings Bond Interest

Accrued interest on Series EE or Series I U.S. savings bonds that you re-deem and use to pay qualified higher education expenses for yourself, your spouse, or a dependent is excluded from income. However, if the redemp-tion proceeds (principal and interest) exceed the qualified higher education expenses, the amount of interest excludable is reduced on a pro rata basis (the accrued interest is multiplied by a fraction whose numerator is the amount of qualified higher education expenses and whose denominator is the amount of redemption proceeds). You can also use the redemption proceeds to fund a qualified tuition program or a Coverdell account.

 Planning Alert The use of savings bond interest to make contributions to Coverdell accounts or qualified tuition programs effectively increases the range of expenses for which the interest can be used. When the interest is used directly to pay educational expenses, the exclusion applies only to amounts used to pay tuition and fees. In contrast, excludable distributions from Coverdell accounts and qualified tuition programs can be used to pay for books, equipment and, in some cases, even room and board. There is a small catch, however. Savings bond interest that is contributed to a qualified tuition program is not treated as a contribution for determining the taxation of program distributions, if that same interest was excluded from the bondholder's income as being used for education expenses.

The exclusion for U.S. savings bond interest is available if your filing status is single, married filing jointly or surviving spouse, or head of household. The exclusion is not available if you are married and file separately.

The exclusion is subject to a phaseout if your modified adjusted gross income for the year of redemption exceeds a specified level. For married taxpayers filing jointly, the phaseout range for 2005 is $91,850-$121,850. The phaseout range for single taxpayers (including heads of households) is $61,200-$76,200. These figures are adjusted annually for inflation.

You must be at least 24 years old on the bond's issue date, which may be earlier than the date on which you buy the bonds. You must also be the sole owner of the bonds or the joint owner with your spouse. The exclusion is not available if you or your spouse are not the original purchaser. For example, if you purchase the bonds and place them in the name of your child, your child cannot claim the exclusion. This benefit is coordinated with other higher education tax benefits. Expenses that are taken into account in a qualified tuition program or Coverdell account cannot be applied to this U.S. savings bond benefit.

 Tax Tip Form 8815, "Exclusion of Interest From Series EE and I U.S. Savings Bonds Issued After 1989 (For Filers With Qualified Higher Education Expenses)," is used to compute the amount of the exclusion. Taxpayers can use Form 8818, "Optional Form To Record Redemption of Series EE and I U.S. Savings Bonds Issued After 1989," to maintain records on redeemed bonds that are necessary to substantiate the interest exclusion for higher education expenses. However, use of the form is not required.

Estimated Tax

If you have income that is not subject to withholding, you may be required to make quarterly estimated tax payments to the IRS. No estimated tax is due unless your estimated tax liability is $1,000 or more.

With careful planning you can keep your estimated tax payments to a minimum without becoming subject to the underpayment penalty. By the same token, if you are headed for an underpayment penalty on your 2005 estimated taxes, it may not be too late to increase your payments to avoid it.

The aim of the estimated tax system is to collect the full amount of your income tax as you go along rather than to wait until after the end of the year. Payments are due quarterly (see Appendix B for due dates) and are based on estimates of the tax that will be due at the end of the year. You may not be required to make estimated tax payments if withholding is credited to your account, but if you have income that is not subject to withholding, these rules may apply to you.

Do You Have to Pay Estimated Tax?

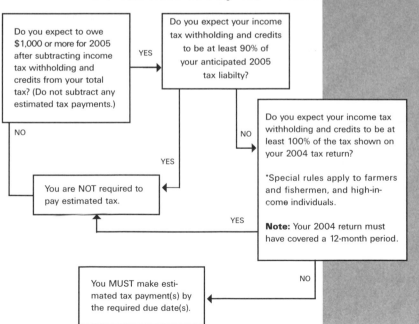

Safe Harbors

You may be subject to penalties if you have not made your estimated tax payments on time or if you have not paid 90% of the year's tax liability by the deadline for the final estimated tax installment. Your final payment is due by January 31, 2006, if you file your return by that date. Alternatively, the final payment is due on January 17, 2006 (January 15, 2006, is a Sunday, and January 16, 2006, is a holiday).

An alternative to the 90% rule may allow you to avoid estimated tax penalties for 2005 if you paid 100% of the tax shown on your 2004 return.

High-Income Taxpayers

If your 2004 adjusted gross income exceeded $150,000 ($75,000 if you were married but filed separately), you are subject to tougher withholding and estimated tax rules. If you fall into this category, you may still avoid the penalty tax by paying 90% of your anticipated 2005 tax liability. (This is the same rule that applies to other taxpayers.) However, if you want to base your estimated tax payments on your 2004 tax liability, you are required to pay 110% of that amount, not just 100%.

In addition to income tax, your estimated tax must cover your self-employment tax, partnership and S corporation income, and any income you receive or are entitled to receive as income from an estate or trust.

 Tax Tip Remember, if you hire someone to care for your children and the care is provided in your home, the IRS will generally consider you an employer. In 2005, if you pay the domestic worker more than $1,400 during the year, you will be liable for the employer's share of FICA tax. You need not withhold federal income tax unless the domestic worker asks you to withhold and you agree. Any tax that you owe because of your employer status is generally reported on Schedule H, "Household Employment Taxes," which is filed with your Form 1040.

Avoiding the Penalties

If you expect to fall short of the required estimated tax payments for 2005, it may not be too late to make additional payments to avoid the penalty. If your installments for the first three quarters were proper and the shortfall is due to increased income in the last quarter, you can make up the entire amount with your final installment. You can also make up a shortfall by having your employer withhold additional amounts before the end of the year. This method is effective for reducing or avoiding penalties for insufficient installments in the earlier quarters of the year because additional withheld tax is treated as coming from all four quarters.

Tax Tip If your income varied considerably during 2005 (e.g., you recognized a large capital gain near the end of the year), you may reduce or eliminate an estimated tax penalty by "annualizing your income." This procedure informs the IRS that you did not receive your income in equal amounts during 2005 and that your estimated payments were based on the amounts actually received during the various periods of the year. To use the annualized method, you must file Form 2210 and Schedule AI with the IRS.

Business Planning

Business tax planning involves not only economic planning for the year at hand, but also making tax-wise decisions that will benefit the business for years to come. Tax-saving strategies must take into account short-term and long-term goals so that decisions made when starting up a particular venture also represent sound tax decisions in following years. Often, because business-planning opportunities must be viewed in conjunction with personal tax planning, you should also take into account individual and investment considerations when making business decisions.

Choosing the Right Business Organization

The first aspect of business planning to be addressed is the choice of business form. This involves selecting among five options: the sole proprietorship, the partnership (general, limited, or limited liability), the C corporation, the S corporation, and the limited liability company (LLC).

(1) A sole proprietorship is an unincorporated business that is owned by one person and has no separate identity apart from its owner. The income and expenses of the business are reported on the owner's individual tax return. Since the liabilities of the business are the owner's personal liabilities, the owner's assets are subject to the risks of the business. For professionals, liability protection can be provided by professional liability insurance.

(2) A partnership is an association of two or more persons to carry on a trade or business. Each partner contributes cash, property or services with the expectation of sharing in the profits and losses of the business. The partnership is not a separate taxable entity and its profits and losses are included on the individual tax returns of the partners. A general partnership provides no asset protection for the partners since creditors of the partnership can attach the personal assets of the partners. However,

the risk of loss to partners in a limited partnership is limited to the amount of capital invested in the partnership.

(3) A C corporation is a separate legal entity organized under state law and created when shareholders transfer cash or property in exchange for stock in the corporation. The profits of the corporation are taxed to both the corporation and also to the shareholders when distributed in the form of dividends. Shareholders cannot deduct any losses incurred by the corporation. Shareholder's liability is limited to the amount of their investment in the corporation. Thus, a shareholder's personal assets are protected from any creditors of the corporation.

Planning Alert Since corporations are solely creatures of state law, the effect of applicable corporate and tax law on a business enterprise is an essential factor in deciding whether to incorporate, where to incorporate and how to operate the corporate entity. As creatures of the state, all corporations are recipients of certain privileges that may be made the basis of taxes as a condition of the grant of those privileges. The privilege of existence and conduct of business that the state of incorporation may grant or withhold as legislative policy dictates, and the privilege of engaging in intrastate business in a foreign state that a foreign state may also grant or withhold in its discretion, subject to federal constitutional limitations, are ordinarily made the basis for taxes and fees, variously designated franchise, privilege or license fees, or taxes.

(4) An eligible domestic corporation can elect to be treated as an S corporation. S corporation shareholders include on their individual tax returns their share of the corporation's separately stated items of income, deduction, loss or credit, and their share of nonseparately stated items of income or loss. S corporation status provides shareholders with the same limited personal liability that is given to C corporation shareholders.

(5) A limited liability company (LLC) is an organization formed under state law that allows limited liability for its members for company obligations and that is usually classified as a partnership for federal income tax purposes. The LLC is not subject to tax; instead, the company income and losses are passed down to its members to be included on their individual tax returns. LLC members also enjoy the same limited personal liability benefit provided to C corporation shareholders.

When a separate legal entity is created, the partnership (whether general, limited, or limited liability) and the LLC afford the most favorable tax consequences to most business organizers. If taxes were the only concern, almost all businesses would be operated in these forms.

Some choices, such as between a general or limited partnership and a C corporation, affect both the legal relationships involved in doing business and the tax consequences. Other choices, however, affect only the legal relationships or the tax consequences, but not both. Thus, the choice between an S corporation and a C corporation affects only taxes. The choice between a general partnership and a limited partnership, however, affects the business relationships among partners and between the partnership and third parties, but generally does not affect the way in which the partnership is taxed. The sole proprietorship, which is an option for a business conducted by a single individual, is not a separate legal entity.

Tax Tip Because a primary business goal is to maximize after-tax income, tax factors play an important part in the choice of business form. In most cases, the tax burden of operating a business through a C corporation is significantly greater than if a "pass-through" entity (a partnership, S corporation or LLC) is used. A C corporation faces double taxation because the corporation must pay income taxes on its income, then, its after-tax income is passed on to its shareholders in the form of dividends and is taxed again to the shareholders. An S corporation or LLC does not encounter double taxation because each is taxed like a partnership where the entity's income passes through to the partners or shareholders, while a sole proprietor's taxable income includes the business's profits. The C corporation usually should be selected only if there are significant advantages that cannot be achieved through a partnership or S corporation.

With the rise of limited liability companies, IRS "check-the-box" regulations for noncorporate entities to elect to be taxed as pass-through entities, and increasingly flexible state statutes, corporations have ceased to become vehicles of choice for many except publicly held entities, entities planning public offerings, or entities that, through compensation or other devices, could regularly report minimal corporate-level tax. The key to the rise of pass-through entities is the avoidance of the corporate-level tax. The price to pay is having all entity-level income passed through to the owners for taxation.

Planning Alert The reduction of individual tax rates, while corporate rates remain the same, has tended to make partnerships and LLCs even more attractive. The reduction in the individual dividend rates to a maximum of 15 percent when the top corporate rate remains at 35 percent still leaves a potential 50-percent tax on income earned at the corporate level. This 15-percent maximum dividend rate applies for tax years 2003 through 2008. With the 15-percent dividend rate potentially applicable even if no corporate-level tax has been paid, however, it is possible that corporate earnings could be taxed at only 15 percent, at the shareholder level, while earnings of pass-through entities are taxed at up to 35 percent at the shareholder level.

The continuing attractiveness of pass-through entities may depend in part, therefore, on the future success corporations have in passing dividends through to shareholders that have not been taxed at the corporate level. If this becomes an established practice, the attractiveness of the corporate format may see resurgence. As long as a sunset hangs over the favorable treatment of dividends, however, it is likely to put a damper on such long-term planning considerations. See Appendix C for the individual tax rate schedules as well as the corporate tax rate brackets.

In most instances, the best entity choice is the one that provides optimal cash flow and the greatest overall amount of long-term, after-tax income. In a family business, it is appropriate to look beyond the first generation and consider the creation of an estate and the management transition to the next generation to ensure survival of the enterprise once it is passed along to the second generation.

Certain concerns are common to all business plans, such as:

Risk. If a business is risky (i.e., when there is inherent exposure to substantial tort or contract liability), and especially if the business owners have substantial wealth outside the business, limiting the potential for personal liability should be addressed.

Finance. All businesses need to raise and manage money. While a large corporation may find it easier than an unincorporated business to borrow money and attract and retain employees, a smaller corporation will experience the same kinds of problems raising capital and attracting staff as do smaller unincorporated organizations. Tax considerations come into play when the owners are also shareholders.

Control. How a business is controlled, and by whom, are key concerns. In a sole proprietorship, the sole proprietor unilaterally controls the affairs of the business enterprise. A partnership must decide how authority is shared among the partners, who makes decisions and what mechanisms are used when partners disagree. A corporation is, theoretically at least, managed by its board of directors. In a corporation with few shareholders, serious conflicts can develop over control of the board.

Continuity. Another universal concern in determining the most appropriate form of business entity is continuity. A sole proprietorship dies with its owner. Generally, the death of a partner does not dissolve the partnership. A corporation (whether S or C) has perpetual existence, and stock can be sold or bequeathed freely. The shares of a public corporation are relatively easy to sell and easy to value, while shares in closely held corporations are less liquid. Under the "check-the-box" regulations, LLCs may choose to be treated as partnerships for federal tax purposes and may adopt operating agreements that ensure continuity of life for the LLC.

Accounting Periods and Methods

The choice of an accounting period over which a business reports its income can be made with tax savings in mind. Most taxpayers follow the calendar year, while some adhere to a fiscal year. However, a choice may not exist for some entities and is severely limited for others, absent a business purpose for the change.

For example, in the case of a sole proprietorship, the business is not a separate entity. Accordingly, all income and losses must be reported for the same accounting period used by the sole proprietor, which is usually a calendar-year period. Partnerships typically have the same tax year as that of its majority partner. Conversely, a C corporation conducting a seasonal business should be on a tax year that includes the entire season.

There are two basic methods of accounting—the cash method and the accrual method. Under the cash method, a business reports its income when it is received and takes deductions when the bills are paid. Under the accrual method, income is accounted for when the right to receive it comes into being, that is, when all the events that determine the right to receive it have occurred. Deductions are taken when all events that determine liability have occurred and the amount of liability can be determined with reasonable accuracy.

A taxpayer whose business transactions during the year are many and complex usually finds the accrual method more desirable because expenses are customarily deducted in the year in which the income to which they relate is reported. Consequently, income tends to be leveled out, thus avoiding income "peaks" that are subject to tax at higher rates. For other taxpayers, the accrual method does not necessarily result in more effective equalization of income than does the cash basis and may even create many unnecessary accounting headaches.

 Planning Alert There are a number of restrictions that apply when evaluating which accounting method to choose. For example, C corporations and partnerships with a corporate partner must use the accrual method. Also, a business that carries inventory must use the accrual method, at least to account for purchases and sales of inventoried merchandise. Depending on the business form chosen, the decision may already be made for you by the Tax Code.

Start-Up Costs

Unlike the costs of running a business, which are currently deductible, expenditures for items of a more permanent nature (i.e., lasting more than a year) generally must be capitalized. Such expenses increase the basis of the property for determining gain or loss on sale or for computing depreciation deductions, if depreciable property is involved. Usually an expenditure is either a currently deductible business expense or a capital expenditure that may be deductible over a period of time. Normally, the business owner has no choice as to how it may be treated.

However, there is a special rule for start-up costs. Effective for amounts paid after October 22, 2004, taxpayers who are considering starting a business may elect to deduct up to $5,000 of start-up expenditures in the tax year in which their trade or business begins. The $5,000 amount, however, must be reduced by the amount of start-up costs that exceed $50,000. If the election is made, start-up expenditures that are not deductible in the year that the trade or business begins must be ratably amortized over 180 months (15 years) beginning in the month that the trade or business begins. Qualified start-up expenses include *any* amount that is paid or incurred in connection with:

(1)   investigating the creation or acquisition of an active trade or business (investigatory expenses are costs incurred in reviewing a prospective business prior to reaching a final decision to acquire or enter that business);

(2)   creating an active trade or business; or

(3)   any activity engaged in for profit and for the production of income before the day on which the active trade or business begins and in anticipation of such activity becoming an active trade or business (i.e., pre-opening costs).

Business start-up expenditures are costs incurred subsequent to the business owner's decision to establish a particular business and prior to the time the business actually begins operating. These costs include: advertising; salaries and wages paid to employees who are being trained and their instructors; travel expenses incurred in lining up prospective distributors, suppliers, or customers; and salaries and fees paid or incurred for executives, consultants and similar professionals.

 Legislation Highlight The election to deduct post-October 22, 2004 start-up costs was enacted under the American Jobs Creation Act of 2004 (P.L. 108-357). For business start-up costs paid or incurred prior to October 23, 2004, an election could be made to amortize start-up costs over a period of not less than 60 months (five years). The new election will benefit smaller businesses that have around $5,000 of start-up expenditures. Larger start-ups, however, will now be required to amortize most or all of these expenses over 15 years rather than the five-year period previously provided. For purposes of determining whether the cumulative cost of start-up expenditures exceeds $50,000, all start-up costs related to a particular trade or business, whether incurred before or after October 22, 2004, are taken into account.

Start-up costs for which a current deduction (and/or 15-year amortization) is not elected are treated as capital expenses and constitute a part of the basis in the business. The increased basis, reflecting the additional start-up costs, will, if the business is sold, reduce gain or increase loss.

 Tax Tip Businesses should avoid any indications that a decision to make an acquisition has been reached, such as instructing a law firm to prepare and submit a letter of intent to purchase, until the latest possible time. The preparation of a letter of intent, even though nonbinding, is indicative that a decision to purchase a particular business has been made and could result in disqualification of later-incurred expenses that would otherwise qualify as deductible (and/or amortizable).

 Tax Tip In addition to the deduction for start-up costs, after October 22, 2004, a corporation may elect to deduct up to $5,000 of organizational expenses it incurs in a tax year in which it begins business. Like start-up costs, the deduction is reduced by the amount of organizational expenses that exceed $50,000. Any remaining balance not immediately deductible must be amortized over a 180-month period (15 years). Organizational expenses are those which are directly related to the creation of the corporation (i.e., incorporation fees, costs for drafting charter and bylaws). Expenses connected with the issuing or selling of stock are not considered organizational expenses.

Retirement Planning as Business Owner

A retirement plan established by an employer for employees may take many forms, such as a pension plan, profit-sharing plan, stock bonus plan, or an annuity plan. Regardless of the type of plan, the primary tax advantages of a retirement plan are twofold: (1) the employee escapes current tax on amounts contributed to the plan and also on income earned on such amounts; and (2) the employer currently deducts its contributions to the plan.

Each type of plan is subject to a variety of restrictions. Some of the restrictions, such as the requirements as to employees who must be covered by the plan, are aimed at protecting employees from being discriminated against by the employer. Other restrictions, such as the limitations on amounts that may be contributed, set ceilings on the tax benefits that the employer and the employee can reap from the plan. Still others, such as the survivor annuity requirements, offer protection to an employee's spouse.

For an employer, the question is whether the advantages, including such nontax advantages as the ability to attract and retain employees, outweigh the statutory and regulatory burdens imposed on such plans.

Types of plans. There are two basic kinds of qualified retirement plans: defined contribution plans and defined benefit plans. Defined contribution plans provide for a separate account for each person covered by the plan. Benefits are based on contributions and the employer agrees to make contributions. These are types of defined contribution plans: 401(k) plans, profit-sharing plans, stock bonus plans, and money purchase pension plans. Defined benefit plans are plans, such as pension and annuity plans, that are not defined contribution plans. In general, contributions to such plans are based on actuarial assumptions that provide for a set benefit for each participant.

There are also several types of plans that have fewer restrictions than defined contribution and defined benefit plans. These include Savings Incentive Match Plan for Employees (SIMPLE) retirement plans and simplified employee pensions (SEPs).

Employing Family Members

When operating a family owned business, you may be faced with the situation of employing your spouse, your children or other relations. When handled properly, these situations can result in significant tax savings.

The wages paid to family members can be deducted as a business expense, just like wages paid to any other employee. To be deductible, the payments must be reasonable and must be for services actually rendered. This makes accurate recordkeeping on the business owner's part essential. In addition, the work performed must be of the type that would generate "ordinary and necessary" business expenses. With these caveats in mind, business owners may be able to shift significant amounts of income to other family members.

 Tax Tip Parents may find that substantial tax savings will result if they can employ their children. This will almost always result in income being shifted from a higher-bracket taxpayer (i.e., the parent) to a lower-bracket taxpayer (i.e., the child). Earned income is not subject to the kiddie tax (see page 89). However, wages paid by a parent to a child who is over 18 and who is employed in the parent's trade or business are subject to Social Security taxes.

Tax Strategies for the Self-Employed

For those individuals with the ambition and courage to start their own business, or for those who are already established as a business owner, the Tax Code offers many opportunities to minimize the tax burden on their hard-earned profits. Year-round tax planning presents opportunities to lower your current tax bill as well as plan for the future. Discussed below are several areas that should be considered whether you are just starting out or have been operating a business for several years.

Medical Expenses

Adequate health and accident insurance is a must in today's economy. For the self-employed individual who purchases their own insurance, they may deduct 100 percent of the premiums paid in 2005 as an adjustment to income on Form 1040. The only limitations on this deduction from gross income are: (1) the amount cannot exceed the net earnings from your business; and (2) you cannot have been eligible to participate in any subsidized health plan of your employer or your spouse's employer.

When calculating your out-of-pocket medical expenses, don't forget that a portion of the premiums for long-term care insurance is a qualified medical expense. The amount that is deductible is limited by the age of the taxpayer. The chart below lists the deductible amounts for the 2005.

In the case of an individual with an attained age before the close of the tax year of:	The limitation is:
40 or less	$270
More than 40 but not more than 50	510
More than 50 but not more than 60	1,020
More than 60 but not more than 70	2,720
More than 70	3,400

Planning Alert An alternative to taking the adjustment to gross income for your accident and health insurance premiums is to employ your spouse in your business. The employment must be real and the necessity substantiated. You can then offer your employee/spouse a medical benefits package. In turn, your spouse names you as a beneficiary under their policy. The result is that the cost of accident and health insurance for you and your family becomes a deductible business expense. Additionally, your spouse can set up a flexible spending account (FSA). This allows your family to set aside pre-tax dollars to cover copayments and medical deductibles.

Health and medical savings accounts. There are a number of other options available in today's marketplace aimed at defraying some of the cost of health and medical related expenses. Such choices include Health Reimbursement Accounts (HRAs), and Flexible Spending Accounts (FSAs). Furthermore, recently created Health Savings Accounts (HSAs) have been available since 2004. The HSAs are similar to the Archer Medical Savings Accounts (MSAs) that taxpayers may enroll in through the end of 2005. With so many options available, it is difficult to assess which plans are appropriate. Below are brief descriptions of the attributes and benefits of each type of plan to assist in determining which plan is most beneficial for your particular needs.

HRAs. An HRA is an employer funded plan that allows employees to pay for medical expenses, health insurance premiums and long-term care, though the employer may establish additional limitations. The employer determines the amount of the annual contribution, but as a general rule, contributions are set below the annual deductible of the accompanying health plan. Any size employer may offer this type of plan.

Reimbursements from an HRA are excluded from the employee's gross income. The unused portion of the account rolls over from year to year, though an employer may restrict the amount of the carryover. However, HRA funds are generally not portable unless permitted by the employer (subject to COBRA provisions). Since these plans are relatively new, there are few current participants. However, qualified HRAs cannot be linked to a deferred compensation arrangement or salary reduction plan. Thus, an HRA cannot be used in conjunction with a cafeteria plan in such a way that the HRA is funded through salary reductions.

Reimbursements from HRAs must be substantiated. The IRS has authorized the use of debit and credit cards for reimbursement purposes. The employee will use the card at authorized service providers for eligible expenses. Presumably this mechanism will aid in meeting the substantiation requirements.

FSAs. In stark contrast to HRAs are FSAs. FSAs are also used to reimburse medical expenses, but not health insurance premiums or long term care. Reimbursements are also excludable from an employee's gross income. Unlike HRAs, FSAs may be offered as part of a cafeteria plan option allowing for contributions to be made on a salary reduction basis, which is the usual route. Employees may also make contributions to an FSA if the FSA is a stand-alone plan.

Under these FSA arrangements, the employee, not the employer, will determine the amount to be contributed to the plan, though employers will often impose a limit. This amount can be altered on an annual basis by the employee. However, any unused contribution cannot be rolled over but instead will be lost if not used by the end of the year. As with HRAs, contributions are not subject to either income or employment taxes such as FICA, Social Security and Medicare.

Like HRAs, FSAs can be established by any size employer and participants may include former employees. Generally, FSAs are not portable, although COBRA extensions may apply in certain situations. In addition, FSAs and HRAs do not have a qualifying health insurance requirement.

HSAs. Recent legislation introduced HSAs, intended to eventually replace Archer MSAs. HSAs, approved as part of the Medicare Prescription Drug, Improvement, and Modernization Act of 2003 (P.L. 108-173), have been allowed since 2004. HSAs enable workers with high-deductible health insurance to make pre-tax contributions to cover health care costs. A high-deductible health plan is a plan that has at least a $1,000 annual deductible for self-only coverage and a $2,000 deductible for family coverage. In addition, annual out-of-pocket expenses paid under the plan must be limited to $5,000 for individuals and $10,000 for families.

The time period for creation of new Archer MSAs, originally scheduled to terminate at the end of 2003, was extended by the Working Families Tax Relief Act of 2004 (P.L. 108-311). New Archer MSAs may be established through the end of 2005.

HSAs and Archer MSAs both allow contributions in 2005 of up to $2,650 for individuals and $5,250 for families. However, an additional deductible contribution is permissible for taxpayers who are age 55 or older who have established an HSA. The additional contribution is limited to $600 in 2005. The limit is then increased by $100 annually through 2009, when the limit will be $1,000.

Planning Alert Taxpayers have little incentive to set up a new Archer MSA in 2005, in light of the availability of HSAs, which differ from MSAs in several ways. In addition to the limited time period for establishing MSAs and the additional contribution available for HSAs. MSAs are available only to individuals working for small employers (50 or fewer employees) or to the self-employed. HSAs have no such restriction. Also, HSAs are available for a wider range of high-deductible plans than are MSAs. For HSAs, a high-deductible plan is one in which the deductible for individuals is $1,000 or $2,000 for a family for 2005. MSAs require $1,750 and $3,500, respectively, for 2005. Further, HSAs allow contributions by the plan participant (and/or the participant's family) and the employer, unlike MSAs, which allow contributions only by the employee *or* the employer (but not both), or the self-employed individual. Finally, a taxpayer may make contributions to an HSA even if the taxpayer has no compensation.

HSAs offer a number of significant tax benefits. Contributions by employees are deductible in determining adjusted gross income, in other words, they are "above-the-line" deductions that may be taken by all taxpayers. Alternately, a contribution by an employer is made on a pre-tax salary reduction basis on behalf of the employee and will also generate a deduction for the employer. Thus, the contribution is tax-free to the employee and tax-deductible to the employer. Employers may offer HSAs either as a stand-alone benefit or through a cafeteria plan.

Distributions from HSAs are also made on a tax-free basis, provided the distributions relate to qualified medical expenses. Expenses generally include costs incurred to diagnose, cure, treat or prevent disease, as well as premiums for long-term care, COBRA and health insurance for those 65 or older or unemployed. Expenses that are not qualified will be treated as taxable income to the recipient and may result in the imposition of a 10 percent excise tax.

Planning Alert Contributions to HSAs grow tax-free and rollover from year to year, allowing a significant build-up as employee's age. In addition, HSAs are portable. Thus, younger employees may build-up large amounts in HSAs and carry those funds with them as they move across jobs throughout their careers. With the rising costs of health care, HSAs likely will be a valuable recruiting tool.

Tax Tip Self-employed individuals should also be aware of state income tax laws. The accident premiums, which are not claimed on the federal return, may be deductible on the state tax return. Be sure to consult with an advisor who is knowledgeable in state income tax law for the state in which you reside.

Automobiles

One of the major expenses of any new or established sole proprietor is operating an automobile. There are several issues to consider which have tax ramifications. Should I buy or lease an automobile? Do I use standard mileage rates or actual expenses? If I use actual expenses, what effect will the business use percentage have on depreciation? What records do I need to maintain to substantiate my automobile deductions? Since your decision on these issues upon acquisition of an automobile has consequences for several years thereafter, the following discussion addresses some of these issues.

Buy vs. Lease

The IRS's decision to allow taxpayers with leased vehicles to use the standard mileage deduction has reduced much of the income tax impact. However, there are still several factors to be considered.

The most important decision is at the time of acquisition of the automobile. An election must be made as between using the standard mileage rate or the actual costs. This is important because not only does it affect how your tax treatment in future years but also the amount of paperwork to substantiate your automobile deduction. If the vehicle is leased, then the election is permanent for the entire lease term (including renewals). If you own the car and elect to use the standard mileage rate the first year, you have the option of changing to actual costs in future years. The only limitation being that you must calculate the vehicle's depreciation using the straight-line method.

Financing a purchase of an automobile will give you an interest deduction from your business income equal to the percentage of business use of the automobile times the yearly interest paid. If you elect to use actual costs, this could result in a substantial deduction from your business income. The downside is that you may be required to make a large down payment and have a large monthly payment. The lease payment has an implicit interest payment, but may not require much of a down payment and has smaller monthly payments.

You do not claim depreciation on a leased car and there is no depreciation recapture when you exchange one leased vehicle for another. Additionally, no basis calculation is necessary to determine gain or loss since there can be no gain or loss with a leased vehicle. However, lessees of luxury autos are subject to special income add-back rules if lease payments are fully deductible to the extent used for business. If a leased, business/investment use automobile with a lease term beginning in 2005 has a fair market value of over $15,200 ($16,700 for trucks and vans and $45,000 for electric automobiles), the lessee must add-back a certain dollar amount to income.

When you purchase an automobile, you must take into consideration depreciation limitations (see below).

Standard Mileage vs. Actual Costs

The standard mileage rate for 2005 is 40.5 cents per mile. The rate does not include the costs of tolls and parking, which are claimed separately. The rate does have a depreciation portion that, if you elect to change to actual cost, is calculated at 17 cents per mile for 2005.

Actual costs include all aspects of operating an automobile, such as gasoline, oil, tires, etc. The main difference between using the standard mileage rate and actual costs is the amount of paperwork required to accurately determine and substantiate your deduction. When exchanging one car for another new car, the basis calculation of the new car could become very complicated if you switched from standard mileage to actual costs.

Vehicle Depreciation

Leased vehicles are not subject to the yearly depreciation limitations imposed by the Tax Code on most purchased vehicles (often referred to as the luxury car limits). The table, below, outlines the depreciation limitations (including the alternative Code Sec. 179 expensing deduction (see page 40)) for purchased nonelectric passenger automobiles (other than trucks, vans or sport utility vehicles (SUVs) placed in service after 2002 and built on a truck chassis).

For Cars Placed in Service		Depreciation Allowable in			
After	Before	Year 1	Year 2	Year 3	Year 4, etc.
12/31/99	1/1/02	3,060*	4,900	2,950	1,775
12/31/01	1/1/04	3,060*	4,900	2,950	1,775
12/31/03	1/1/05	2,960*	4,800	2,850	1,675
12/31/04	1/1/06	2,960	4,700	2,850	1,675

* The depreciation deduction first-year limitation was increased if either the 30-percent or 50-percent bonus depreciation was elected. To qualify for bonus depreciation, the vehicle had to have been purchased after September 10, 2001, and placed in use before January 1, 2005.

Trucks and vans (including SUVs and minivans built on a truck chassis) that have a gross vehicle weight of 6,000 pounds or less are subject to their own set of depreciation limitations if placed in service after 2002. These caps, as shown in the table below, reflect the higher costs associated with such vehicles.

For Trucks and Vans Placed in Service		Depreciation Allowable in			
		Year 1	Year 2	Year 3	Year 4, etc.
After	Before				
12/31/02	1/1/04	3,360*	5,400	3,250	1,975
12/31/03	1/1/05	3,260*	5,300	3,150	1,875
12/31/04	1/1/06	3,260	5,200	3,150	1,875

* The depreciation deduction first-year limitation was increased if either the 30-percent or 50-percent bonus depreciation was elected. To qualify for bonus depreciation, the vehicle had to have been purchased after September 10, 2001, and placed in use before January 1, 2005.

 Tax Tip A separate set of depreciation limitations apply to electric passenger cars built by an original equipment manufacturer and used in a trade or business after August 5, 1997 and before 2007.

 Tax Tip Trucks and vans (including SUVs and minivans built on a truck chassis) that have a gross vehicle weight greater than 6,000 pounds are not subject to any of the above depreciation limitations. Thus, if you purchase an SUV for your trade or business and use the vehicle 100 percent for business, you may deduct the full amount of allowable depreciation for the year if it has a gross vehicle weight in excess of 6,000 pounds. (However, see, below, regarding the $25,000 Code Sec. 179 expensing cap on SUVs (and certain trucks and vans) that are exempt from the depreciation limitations.) Also exempted from the luxury car limits are certain trucks and vans placed in service after July 6, 2003, if, because of their design, they are not likely to be used for personal purposes.

 Legislation Highlight Under the American Jobs Creation Act of 2004 (P.L. 108-357), the maximum amount of the cost of an SUV that a business owner may expense under Code Sec. 179 is reduced to $25,000, effective for SUVs placed in service after October 22, 2004. This rule applies to SUVs, trucks with a cargo load shorter than six feet, and passenger vans that seat less than 10 behind the driver's seat and that are exempt from the depreciation caps (i.e., have a gross vehicle weight greater than 6,000 pounds). Previously, these vehicles could be expensed up to the $100,000 (indexed for inflation) limitation applicable to other business assets (see page 40).

Note that owners of heavy SUVs will still recoup much more of their investment in the first year than they will for a car that is subject to the luxury car limits. The full cost of a pick-up truck with a cargo bed at least six feet long can still be expensed (up to $105,000 for 2005) under Code Sec. 179.

Example. In January 2005, Alex purchases a new Ford Expedition for use in his landscaping business. He will use it 100 percent for business. The cost of the Expedition is $45,000. Its gross vehicle weight, as rated by Ford, is 7,000 pounds. By definition, it is not a luxury car, and Alex may claim a first-year deduction of up to $9,000 as his depreciation expense ($45,000 x 20%).

Alternatively, Alex may claim a first-year deduction for the SUV of up to $29,000. This includes a Code Sec. 179 expensing deduction of $25,000 and a normal first-year depreciation deduction of $4,000 (($45,000 - $25,000) x 20%). Before he decides which option to elect, he will need to discuss other tax considerations with his tax advisor.

 Tax Tip Carefully picking assets for use in Code Sec. 179 expensing is a worthwhile strategy to maximize tax savings. The election to expense may be applied against the entire cost or a portion of the cost of one or more assets. To accelerate deductions, it is generally preferable to allocate the expense allowance to assets with the longest recovery period.

Substantiation

To successfully claim a deduction for an automobile, substantial record-keeping is required. The following information should be retained for each automobile for at least four years after it is removed from service:

- purchase bill-of-sale or lease contract;
- receipts for all maintenance and repairs;
- total mileage driven each year broken down into personal, commuting, and business miles; and
- dates of each use for business with the purpose of the expense.

To achieve adequate substantiation of your automobile expenses, a daily log or diary should be kept. Odometer readings should be entered with each trip, although multiple short trips may be combined. Entries should be made when gasoline, oil, or any other purchase is made. Maintaining this type of record will make determining your deduction quick and accurate at tax time. Plus, in the event of an audit, you will easily be able to substantiate your deduction.

Travel and Entertainment

An often overlooked deduction are those expenses incurred for moving, travel away from your tax home and entertainment of clients.

Moving Expenses

For the expenses of moving to qualify as a deduction from gross income, three tests must be satisfied. The requirements are distance, commencement of work and employment period after the move.

Distance test. This test requires that the distance between the taxpayer's new place of employment and his former home be at least 50 miles greater than the distance from his former employer's place of business and his former home. The shortest possible route, not the actual route taken by the taxpayer, measures the distance.

Commencement of work test. The purpose of the move must be to: (1) start your first job or begin a new job after a period of unemployment; (2) begin work for a new employer; or (3) begin work at a new location for the same employer. The move must take place within a reasonable time to the commencement of work.

Employment post-move test. For employees, this requirement is met by working 39 weeks out of the next 52 weeks following the move. However, for the self-employed, the requirement is slightly more complex. A self-employed person must work 78 weeks out of the next 104 weeks, with 39 weeks being worked in the first 52-week period.

 Tax Tip You may claim your moving expenses before actually meeting the employment post-move test. If you reasonably anticipate satisfying the requirement, you may deduct the qualified moving expenses in the year of the move. In the event you later do not meet the requirement, then you should file an amended return paying tax on the now nondeductible moving expenses.

If you pass these three tests, then your qualified moving expenses are deductible. Qualified moving expenses are defined as the reasonable charges incurred for transportation of your household goods and yourself to the new location. The transportation of household goods also includes storage of up to 30 days prior to or just after the move. In the cost of transporting yourself, lodging may be included but not meals. The mileage rate for use of an automobile or truck is 15 cents per mile for 2005 or actual costs. Tolls and parking are claimed separately.

Travel Away From Home

A wide variety of expenses are deductible when one must travel away from one's tax home for business reasons. One's tax home being defined as either the regular or principal place of business or, if no principal place of business exists, one's regular and principal place of abode. Deductible expenses include all transportation costs (for example, roundtrip airfare and the cost of getting around at your destination whether by taxi or rental car), lodging, cleaning, communications, meals and tips associated with these services (for special rules on meals, see below). These expenses are deductible only for yourself, you may not include a spouse or dependent. Additionally, if any part of the trip is for pleasure, you must prorate the expenses between business and pleasure.

 Tax Tip The deductibility of travel expenses is another reason why employing one's spouse can be beneficial. If the spouse's presence fills a legitimate business need, then the cost of the spouse accompanying you on your business trip as an employee of your business will be fully deductible. However, as before, if any part of the trip is recreational, you will still need to prorate the expenses for both of you between business and pleasure. Keep in mind that the costs of your return to your tax home will still be deductible even if you take a vacation following a business trip.

Work Assignments. If a temporary work assignment keeps you away from home, the costs of staying at the temporary work site are deductible. Temporary work assignment is defined as being an assignment for less than one year. Anything longer than one year is an indefinite work assignment where travel and living expenses are not deductible. The exception being for government workers who the Attorney General certifies need to be away from their tax homes for longer than one year but are on a temporary assignment.

Substantiation. Accurate recordkeeping is necessary to document your expenses while traveling away from your tax home. Receipts for all expenses must be kept and you should record the nature of the business conducted which relate to the incurring of the expense. There is an alternative that reduces the amount of recordkeeping required. For meals, lodging and incidental expenses, one can use the federal per diem rates, also known as the M&IE rates. By using these rates while traveling away from home, the only required substantiation is the lodging bill and a record of the business conducted, even in the event you are audited.

Tax Tip Even though the use of the M&IE rates reduces the amount of recordkeeping required to claim deductible travel expenses, one must be aware of the fact that the federal government, based on averages for the area, sets these rates. Thus, your actual costs may be higher than the M&IE rates. The additional expenses may be taken as an itemized deduction for unreimbursed travel expenses subject to the two percent of adjusted gross income limitation.

Per diem rates. These are rates set by the federal government to cover the costs of meals, incidental expenses and lodging in all areas of the United States. The rate tables are constantly updated. They are available in print as well as on the Internet at http://www.gsa.gov/. The rates may be used for just meals and incidentals, just lodging, together, or in a special high-low method.

Foreign travel. Since many of today's business opportunities are of a global nature, travel outside the United States is a real possibility. There are special requirements for determining whether travel expenses incurred outside the United States are deductible. Obviously, if 100 percent of the travel and expenses are for business purposes, they are fully deductible. However, if any portion of your time outside the United States is for personal pleasure, then you may have to prorate your expenses between business and personal. Prior to any trip outside the United States, a review of the nature of the trip and the special rules governing deduction of business travel expenses should be undertaken with your tax advisor.

Meals and Entertainment

The expenses of meals and entertainment must be directly related to and associated with your trade or business. Those expenses that qualify are then subject to a limitation of 50 percent. "Directly related" is defined as an activity in which the taxpayer had a general expectation of deriving a business benefit during the entertainment activity. "Associated with" allows for activities immediately preceding or following the business activity. Care should be taken to substantiate the dates, times, those in attendance and the purpose of the meals and entertainment.

 Tax Tip The price of tickets to popular sporting or theatrical events obtained through a legal ticket broker will not be entirely deductible. Only the face value of the ticket is a deductible expense for income tax purposes. Thus, to pay $1,000 for a box seat at a popular musical with a face value of $250 will only net you a deduction of $250.

Home Office

For many small businesses, the garage or bedroom of the home is the main office. The Tax Code allows you to deduct your trade or business expenses incurred in your home office. You may have heard that Congress has simplified the rules for claiming a deduction for using a home office. However, there are other tax considerations to take into account before you decide to claim your home office deduction.

The requirements to qualify a home office to enable you to deduct the allocable expenses are:

(1)   the office must be used exclusively and regularly as a principal place of business;

(2)   as a place of business that is used in meeting or dealing with customers in the usual course of business; or

(3)   in connection with the individual's business if the individual is using a separate structure that is appurtenant to, but not attached to, the home.

A principal place of business requirement includes use of the home office to conduct administrative or management activities for your trade or business, if there is no other fixed location of the trade or business where the taxpayer conducts substantial administrative or management activities of the trade or business.

Although this allows more people, along with the exception for storage of inventory, to claim the home office deduction, they must still meet the regular and exclusive standard. "Exclusively" means that no personal activity is allowed in the area set aside for business use. "Regular" means that the business activities must be consistent and ongoing, not sporadic.

Deductible expenses. There are two types of expenses that are deductible under the home office deduction, indirect and direct expenses. Direct expenses are those directly related to the conduct of the trade or business. This includes any cost to maintain the area specifically set aside as the home office. Indirect expenses are those expenses that are incurred in operating the home, such as the utilities, insurance, real estate taxes and mortgage interest. The portion of these expenses that can be claimed as an expense is determined by comparing the square footage used for the home office to the entire usable living space.

The expenses also include a deduction for depreciation of the home office area. However, you must deduct your expense in a specific order. Your total deductions cannot exceed your total income from your trade or business. The specific order for deducting your home office expenses is:

(1)   expenses that are required by the business but are not allocable to the use of the home;

(2)   expenses that would be deductible if the individual did not use the home for business purposes, such as real estate taxes and mortgage interest;

(3) household expenses that are allocable to the business use of the home; and

(4) depreciation expenses.

Under no circumstances can the deductions for items 2, 3, and 4 exceed your total income and generate a loss for your trade or business. However, unused deductions from items 3 and 4 may be carried over to future years, but again subject to the same income limitations for taking the home office deduction.

Tax Tip Real estate taxes and mortgage interest are always deductible whether a business or personal expenditure. If your business does not generate enough income to deduct the home office portion of real estate taxes and mortgage interest from you business expenses, you can still deduct the full amount of taxes and interest on your Schedule A, Form 1040.

Planning Alert Before taking the home office deduction, one should determine the tax consequence on the sale of the home. The portion allocated as your home office will not qualify for the exclusion of capital gains on the sale of a principal residence if the business use of the property takes place in a separate structure (e.g. a detached garage). Since you are required to allocate the sale gain between residential and business use in such a case, the capital gains tax on your sale of the business portion of the home may be larger than the total depreciation deductions that you benefited from in prior years. In such a case, a home office deduction may not generate a net tax advantage over time.

Although allocation of gain is not required when both the business and residential uses take place in the same structure (e.g. where the home office is in an extra bedroom within the home), any depreciation expense related to that business use is recognized upon the sale. It would seem that such gain would be recognized as ordinary income to the extent it represents accelerated depreciation recapture, with the remainder recognized as capital gain.

Tax Tip You should also be aware that there are special rules for determining the portion of the indirect expense that may be claimed for operating a day care center in your home. Application of these rules could result in a greater home office deduction and a lower tax liability.

Office equipment. You are allowed a deduction for the purchase and maintenance of equipment necessary for the conduct of your trade or business. This usually takes the form of a depreciation allowance. You may, under certain circumstance, take an expense deduction of up to $105,000 for 2005 under Code Sec. 179 for the purchase of equipment for your trade or business. See page 40.

One of the major assets for any business is a computer. The general rule is that you can elect to take a Code Sec. 179 expense deduction for the cost of the computer if:

- the computer is used 100 percent for the trade or business; and
- the home office meets the requirements as a home office.

In the event the computer is not used exclusively for business, then you must determine the business use percentage of the computer, which will determine whether you can expense or depreciate the equipment.

Another issue that is facing many self-employed individuals is how to handle the costs of software needed to operate the business and to build and maintain a web site. The IRS allows purchased software to be depreciated over a three-year period. Other costs of software may be capitalized and depreciated or expensed as long as the business accounts for all such costs in a consistent manner. The IRS has not made any definitive statement as of this writing regarding the handling of web site development and maintenance. You would be advised to consult with a tax advisor prior to claiming any deduction with relation to a web site for your trade or business.

 Tax Tip You can take a Code Sec. 179 expense deduction for off-the-shelf computer software for 2005 through 2007. This deduction, which had been scheduled to expire after 2005, was extended by the American Jobs Creation Act of 2004 (P.L. 108-357).

Depending on your cash flow and other factors, you may decide to depreciate your computer and electronic equipment. The general depreciation schedule for this type of equipment is over five years with larger amounts being taken in earlier years. For desks, filing cabinets and chairs, the general depreciation schedule covers seven years.

Retirement Plans

There are several plans that self-employed individuals can establish, which will allow them to make maximum contributions and offer their employees a retirement benefit plan.

Simplified Employee Pensions (SEPs)

A SEP plan is one of the more common types of retirement plans used by self-employed people because of its simplicity of administration coupled with the potential to contribute more than other more complex plans. A self-employed individual may contribute up to the lesser of 25 percent of the net earnings from the trade or business or $42,000 for 2005. The maximum amount of compensation that can be considered for 2005 is $210,000.

Contributions to a SEP can be made up until the time of the filing of the return including extensions. This also applies to actually establishing the SEP account. SEPs, however, are the only plan that allows this kind of post-year end planning.

 Tax Tip Although you can wait until April 15 (or later, if an extension is requested) to make your SEP contribution, the sooner you make the contribution the better off you will be at retirement. The extra interest earned can be substantial thanks to the wonders of compound interest. For more information, you should check with your financial advisor. However, for all retirement plans (not just the SEPs), your business must have net earnings to be able to make these contributions.

Keogh Plans

Keogh plans are qualified retirement plans that self-employed individuals establish for themselves and their employees either as a defined contribution or a defined benefit plan. The defined contribution plan may be either a profit-sharing plan or a money purchase plan. The maximum contribution limitations for a defined contribution plan in 2005 are the lesser of $42,000 or 100 percent of the participant's compensation. The maximum amount of compensation for a defined benefit plan for 2005 is limited to the lesser of $170,000 or 100 percent of the participant's average compensation for three consecutive calendar years.

 Tax Tip Remember that you can make a contribution to a Keogh plan as late as April 15th (or later if an extension has been filed) but the plan has to be established by December 31st of the prior year. Thus, to make a contribution on April 17th of 2006 (April 15, 2006, is a Saturday) for 2005, the Keogh plan must have been established by December 31, 2005.

 Planning Alert In practice, determining the maximum contribution to a defined contribution plan is a more complicated procedure than just applying the above formula to the individual's net income from self-employment. The complexity arises from the fact that certain adjustments have to be made to net income before the formula can be applied. A discussion of the required adjustments is beyond the scope of this publication. If you are a self-employed individual who is interested in funding a defined contribution plan, you should seek the necessary guidance from your tax preparer.

The tax treatment of the benefits that you will receive from your Keogh plan after you reach 59½ depends upon the type of benefits you will receive. The benefits are taxed either as an annuity (that is, periodic payments over a period of time) or as a lump-sum distribution. If you receive a lump-sum distribution, you may generally escape immediate taxation on the amount distributed by rolling the distribution over into a traditional IRA, or, in some situations another employer's retirement plan

Savings Incentive Match Plan for Employees (SIMPLE)

The SIMPLE is a type of plan aimed at small businesses to encourage the establishment of retirement plans for employers and employees. This was accomplished by establishing a few simple rules. Two forms of the plan exist—a 401(k) type plan and an IRA type plan. To qualify for establishing a SIMPLE plan, the business must have 100 or fewer employees who receive at least $5,000 in compensation in the previous year and no other retirement plan has been established. The maximum contribution that can be made to a SIMPLE plan for 2005 is $10,000. Additionally, for those who are 50 years or older, an extra $2,000 may be contributed in 2005. This catch-up amount increases to $2,500 for 2006 and later. Finally, since these plans are to encourage retirement benefits and savings, the employer is required to make a matching contribution to a SIMPLE account of one to three percent of the employee's compensation.

 Tax Tip Here is another example of the benefits of employing your spouse. As your own employee, you can offer a benefits package that includes a retirement plan. You will then be able to shelter more of your business' net earnings in a tax preferred account increasing the family wealth at retirement.

Individual Retirement Account (IRA)

A self-employed person may establish an individual retirement account. You will be able to contribute up to $4,000 per year for 2005, 2006 and 2007, which is taken as a deduction on your Form 1040. In 2008 and thereafter, the maximum contribution amount will become $5,000, which will be inflation adjusted starting in 2009. Additionally, for those over 50 years of age, a catch-up provision is available. You may contribute up to an additional $500 for 2005, which increases to $1,000 for 2006 and thereafter. You are not considered a participant in a plan merely because your spouse is an active participant in an employer sponsored retirement plan. However, the maximum contribution amount is phased out at adjusted gross income between $150,000 and $160,000 (jointly computed) if you are not an active participant in an employer sponsored retirement plan, but your spouse is an active participant. A financial advisor should be consulted prior to establishing and contributing to an IRA.

Tax Tip One should consider making contributions to a traditional IRA during a period of slowly reducing tax rates. The increasing contribution amounts allow you to shelter more of your income from the current higher rates. Once the rates have been reduced, you can convert your traditional IRA to a Roth IRA. You will have to pay income tax on all your contributions to date, but the taxation will be at the new lower rate. This will result in a lower tax liability. However, one must take care that your income level does not increase to the point where you will be disqualified from making the conversion to a Roth IRA. Consultation with a tax advisor is strongly recommended before you take any action.

This is just a brief overview to expose the self-employed person to the numerous retirement plans available. There are many rules and regulations that govern the establishment and administration of each of these plans. Prior to opening a retirement account, it is important to discuss with your financial advisor your financial goals and your retirement expectation in order to establish a plan most suited to your needs and the needs of your trade or business.

Taxation

Several strategies have been discussed to lower your net earnings prior to determining your taxable income. The reality of the situation is that you will owe income, Social Security and Medicare, and unemployment taxes. Since you are self-employed, you do not have an employer withholding for these taxes from your wages or making a contribution on your behalf. You must remember that our current method of taxation is pay as you earn the income. This will require you to make estimated tax payments on a quarterly basis. These payments must include enough to cover your income and Social Security and Medicare obligations, otherwise you could incur severe penalties. For a detailed discussion of estimated taxes, see page 105.

Self-Employment Tax

The self-employment tax is the imposition of Social Security and Medicare taxes on the self-employed. The components of the tax are 12.4 percent for Social Security (also known as OASDI or old age survivors and disability insurance) and 2.9 percent for the Medicare (also known as hospital insurance). Social Security is imposed on the first $90,000 of income earned in 2005. There is no income limitation on the Medicare taxation. The income limitation is inflation adjusted. The important concept to remember is that as a self-employed person, you are both the employer and employee. Thus, where employed workers only pay one half of the Social Security and Medicare taxes and the employer pays the other half, you, the self-employed, must pay the whole amount. To help relieve the burden of this tax, you are allowed to deduct one half of the amount of self-employed tax from your gross income on the adjustments to income section of the Form 1040.

Alternative Minimum Tax (AMT)

The alternative minimum tax was imposed by Congress to ensure that all taxpayers, including the wealthy, paid at least some tax. Over time this tax, whose amounts are not inflation-adjusted, has moved lower on the economic scale to affect more middle-income people. This tax is imposed by adding back into your gross income certain preferences and adjustments. Self-employed people must be aware of the effect on their tax liability of adjustments for accelerated depreciation on assets. This will also affect the taxation of the gain or loss from the disposition of these assets. Frequent consultations with your tax or financial advisor are strongly encouraged to avoid surprises at tax time when it may be too late to avoid the ramifications of your decisions. A more-detailed discussion of the AMT is provided at page 12.

Employee v. Independent Contractor

Your endeavors as a self-employed individual may lead you into the murky area of employee classification. The classification of an individual as an employee or as an independent contractor affects both the worker and the employer. A primary consequence of this determination is responsibility for employment taxes. If a worker is an employee, then the employer is liable for the employer share of FICA tax and must withhold the employee's share and income tax as well. If the worker is an independent contractor, then he or she is responsible for payment of self-employment tax.

The underlying determination is based on control—how much control does the employer exercise over the worker? The IRS looks to three types of control, namely behavioral control, financial control and the relationship of the parties. The IRS has listed 20 factors it uses when making a determination about worker status.

(1) *Instructions.* A worker who is required to comply with other persons' instructions about when, where, and how he or she is to work is ordinarily an employee. This control factor is present if the person or persons for whom the services are performed have the right to require compliance with instructions.

(2) *Training.* Training a worker by requiring an experienced employee to work with the worker, by corresponding with the worker, by requiring the worker to attend meetings, or by using other methods, indicates that the person or persons for whom the services are performed want the services performed in a particular method or manner.

(3) *Integration.* Integration of the worker's services into the business operations generally shows that the worker is subject to direction and control. When the success or continuation of a business depends to an appreciable degree upon the performance of certain services, the workers who perform those services must necessarily be subject to a certain amount of control by the owner of the business.

(4) *Services Rendered Personally.* If the services must be rendered personally, presumably the person or persons for whom the services are performed are interested in the methods used to accomplish the work as well as in the results.

(5) *Hiring, Supervising, and Paying Assistants.* If the person or persons for whom the services are performed hire, supervise, and pay assistants, that factor generally shows control over the workers on the job. However, if one worker hires, supervises, and pays the other assistants pursuant to a contract under which the worker agrees to provide materials and labor and under which the worker is responsible only for the attainment of a result, this factor indicates an independent contractor status

(6) *Continuing Relationship.* A continuing relationship between the worker and the person or persons for whom the services are performed indicates that an employer-employee relationship exists. A continuing relationship may exist where work is performed at frequently recurring although irregular intervals.

(7) *Set Hours of Work.* The establishment of set hours of work by the person or persons for whom the services are performed is a factor indicating control.

(8) *Full Time Required.* If the worker must devote substantially full time to the business of the person or persons for whom the services are performed, such person or persons have control over the amount of time the worker spends working and impliedly restrict the worker from doing other gainful work. An independent contractor, on the other hand, is free to work when and for whom he or she chooses.

(9) *Doing Work on Employer's Premises.* If the work is performed on the premises of the person or persons for whom the services are performed, that factor suggests control over the worker, especially if the work could be done elsewhere. Work done off the premises of the person or persons receiving the services, such as at the office of the worker, indicates some freedom from control.

(10) *Order or Sequence Set.* If a worker must perform services in the order or sequence set by the person or persons for whom the services are performed, that factor shows that the worker is not free to follow

the worker's own pattern of work but must follow the established routines and schedules of the person or persons for whom the services are performed.

(11) *Oral or Written Reports.* A requirement that the worker submit regular or written reports to the person or persons for whom the services are performed indicates a degree of control.

(12) *Payment by Hour, Week, Month.* Payment by the hour, week, or month generally points to an employer-employee relationship, provided that this method of payment is not just a convenient way of paying a lump sum agreed upon as the cost of a job. Payment made by the job or on a straight commission generally indicates that the worker is an independent contractor.

(13) *Payment of Business and/or Traveling Expenses.* If the person or persons for whom the services are performed ordinarily pay the worker's business and/or traveling expenses, the worker is ordinarily an employee. An employer, to be able to control expenses, generally retains the right to regulate and direct the worker's business activities.

(14) *Furnishing of Tools and Materials.* The fact that the person or persons for whom the services are performed furnish significant tools, materials, and other equipment tends to show the existence of an employer-employee relationship.

(15) *Significant Investment.* If the worker invests in facilities that are used by the worker in performing services and are not typically maintained by employees (such as the maintenance of an office rented at fair value from an unrelated party), that factor tends to indicate that the worker is an independent contractor. On the other hand, lack of investment in facilities indicates dependence on the person or persons for whom the services are performed for such facilities and, accordingly, the existence of an employer-employee relationship. Special scrutiny is required with respect to certain types of facilities, such as home offices.

(16) *Realization of Profit or Loss.* A worker who can realize a profit or suffer a loss as a result of the worker's services (in addition to the profit or loss ordinarily realized by employees) is generally an independent contractor, but the worker who cannot is an employee.

(17) *Working for More Than One Firm at a Time.* If a worker performs more than de minimis services for a multiple of unrelated persons or firms at the same time, that factor generally indicates that the worker is an independent contractor. However, a worker who performs services for more than one person may be an employee of each of the persons, especially where such persons are part of the same service arrangement.

(18) *Making Service Available to General Public.* The fact that a worker makes his or her services available to the general public on a regular and consistent basis indicates an independent contractor relationship.

(19) *Right to Discharge.* The right to discharge a worker is a factor indicating that the worker is an employee and the person possessing the right is an employer. An employer exercises control through the threat of dismissal, which causes the worker to obey the employer's instructions. An independent contractor, on the other hand, cannot be fired so long as the independent contractor produces a result that meets the contract specifications.

(20) *Right to Terminate.* If the worker has the right to end his or her relationship with the person for whom the services are performed at any time he or she wishes without incurring liability, that factor indicates an employer-employee relationship.

International Tax Planning

As the world continues to shrink under the impact of technological change and business growth, the movement of individuals between countries is rapidly accelerating. One of the most harrowing and treacherous issues confronting individuals when they relocate abroad temporarily (or permanently) is the tax treatment they will be accorded when leaving their home country and starting life under an unfamiliar tax regime.

Forward-looking tax planning is critical before moving in order to optimize opportunities and avoid unnecessary tax costs. The in-transit hiatus between one country and another can represent a once-in-a-lifetime chance for locking in tax-free profits or putting in place structures to minimize future tax liabilities. Every international promotion, transfer or migration is an event requiring analysis from the viewpoint of its tax consequences in both the taxpayer's old and new country of residence.

 Planning Alert The scope of international tax planning is too vast to cover in a publication of this type. The following discussion outlines some key concepts and raises some key issues that need to be addressed with your tax advisor should the opportunity present itself to work or live abroad.

Overview of U.S. Jurisdiction

The United States taxes the worldwide income of those individuals and entities over which it maintains personal jurisdiction such as U.S. citizens, residents, and domestic corporations, regardless of where the income is earned. For example, if a U.S. citizen lives in France and earns income in France, the U.S. has the right to tax that income. Similarly, if a domestic corporation chartered in Delaware earns income directly through a branch in Brazil, the U.S. has the right to tax that income.

When the U.S. taxes the non-U.S. income (called

foreign-source income) of those individuals and entities over which it has personal jurisdiction, that same income is also usually taxed in the other country, resulting in double taxation. Since such double taxation discourages international trade, the U.S. utilizes tax treaties and foreign tax credits to eliminate or at least mitigate this overlapping taxation, typically conceding that the country where the income is earned has the primary jurisdiction to tax the foreign income.

In addition to taxing U.S. citizens and domestic entities, the United States also taxes the income of individuals and entities over which it does not maintain personal jurisdiction, such as nonresident aliens and foreign corporations. However, since such individuals and entities do not have a personal connection (or nexus) with the United States, they are only taxed by the U.S. on the U.S-source income they receive. For this purpose, income that is effectively connected with a U.S. trade or business is taxed in the same manner as if received by a U.S. citizen or domestic entity. Nonbusiness income from U.S. sources (i.e., fixed and determinable, annual or periodic income) is subject to a flat tax rate and collected through withholding.

Sourcing Rules

Whether income is derived from U.S. or foreign sources is not only important to nonresident aliens and foreign corporations, but also to U.S. citizens and domestic entities for purposes of determining the amount of foreign tax credit that may be claimed. The determination of the source of income is made based on the following types of incomes.

(1) *Interest Income.* In determining the source of income as U.S. or foreign, the location of the debtor of the note determines the source of the income. If the debtor is a U.S. resident or domestic corporation, it is U.S.-source income; if the debtor is a foreign resident or a foreign corporation, it is foreign-source income.

(2) *Dividends.* In characterizing the source of income as U.S. or foreign, the location of the payor of the dividend determines the source of the income. If the payor is a domestic corporation, it is U.S.-source income. If the payor is a foreign corporation, it is foreign-source income.

(3) *Services.* In classifying the source of income as U.S. or foreign, the location of where the services are performed determines the source of the income. If services are performed in the U.S., the income is considered U.S.-source income; if they are performed outside the U.S., it is foreign-source income.

(4) *Rents and Royalties.* In determining the source of income as U.S. or foreign, the location of where the property is used determines the source of the income. If the property is used in the U.S., it is considered U.S.-source income; if used outside the U.S., it is considered foreign-source income.

(5) *Gain on Sale of Real Property.* The location of the property determines the source of the income. If the property is located in the U.S., it is considered U.S.-source income; if located outside the U.S., it is foreign-source income.

(6) *Gain on the Sale of Securities.* In categorizing the source of income as U.S. or foreign, the residency of the seller determines the source of the income. If the seller of the security is a U.S. resident, it is considered U.S.-source income; if the seller is a foreign resident, it is foreign-source income.

Deductions are allowed for expenses and losses directly related to either U.S.- or foreign-source gross income, as well as a ratable portion of expenses and losses that are not definitely related to any specific item of gross income. The allocation and apportionment of deductions only has significance in limited instances, such as when the taxable income is calculated on the net amount of income effectively connected with the conduct of a U.S. trade or business. The rules do not have any effect in cases in which a foreign person's only connection to the U.S. is as a passive investor deriving U.S.-source nonbusiness income, since such income is taxed on a gross basis through a flat withholding rate.

A deduction is properly allocated to a class of gross income if the deduction is related to the activity or property from which the gross income is derived. The apportionment of the deduction must reasonably reflect the factual relationship between the deduction and the gross income. The key is that the deduction should be apportioned properly between U.S. and foreign operations. In order to aid taxpayers in what can often be a difficult task, special apportionment rules are provided which cover items such as interest expense, research and development expenditures, losses from the disposition of property and other specialized items of expense.

Income of Foreign Persons and Entities

Activities that subject foreign persons to U.S. tax can be grouped into two general categories: (1) U.S.-source nonbusiness income; and (2) U.S. trade or business profits.

U.S.-source nonbusiness income. Foreign persons will be taxed at a flat 30-percent rate on U.S.-source fixed or determinable periodical income which is not effectively connected with the conduct of a U.S. trade or business. Periodical income may include interest, dividends, rents, salaries, wages, premiums, annuities, and other fixed or determinable annual or periodical gains, profits and income. Generally, however, the U.S. exempts from taxation portfolio interest income and capital gains, except for gains on the sale of U.S. real property interests which is taxed as income effectively connected with a U.S. trade or business.

U.S. trade or business income. If a nonresident individual or foreign corporation is engaged in a trade or business within the U.S., the net amount of income effectively connected with the conduct of that U.S. trade or business is taxed at the regular graduated income tax rates.

In determining whether income is "effectively connected" with a U.S. trade or business, two factors are considered: (1) whether the income is derived from assets used in, or held for use in, the conduct of a U.S. business; and (2) whether the activity of the U.S. business was a material factor in the realization of the income.

 **Planning Alert** Due regard is given to the treatment of the asset or income given in the books that are kept for the U.S. business, but this, alone, is not a controlling factor.

Use or holding factor. The use or holding factor is especially important in the case of income of a passive nature (such as dividends) when business activities are not likely to be a direct or material contributor to the realization of income. In general, an asset held for the principal purpose of promoting the conduct of the U.S. business is to be considered held for use in such business, making the income derived from the asset effectively connected with the business.

 Example A foreign corporation that is engaged in paper pulp manufacturing in the U.S. purchases stock in a domestic lumber corporation in order to ensure a constant source of supply of materials. The dividend income from the lumber stock, and any gain realized from selling the stock, is income effectively connected with the foreign corporation's U.S. business. The foreign corporation is, therefore, taxed in the same manner as a domestic corporation on this income.

Assets arising in the ordinary course of the trade or business, such as accounts receivable, are also considered to be used or held for use in that trade or business. The same is true of other assets held in a direct relationship to the trade or business. In determining whether a direct relationship exists, primary consideration is to be given to the connection between the asset and the present needs, as distinguished from the future needs, of the U.S. business.

Business activity factor. The business activity factor ordinarily is applied in cases in which income arises directly from the active conduct of the taxpayer's trade or business in the United States. The test is of primary significance when, for example: (a) dividends, interest, etc., are derived by a dealer in stocks or securities; (b) royalties are derived in the active conduct of a business involving the licensing of patents or other intangibles; or (c) fees are derived in the active conduct of a servicing business. Activity related to the management of investments is not treated as directly related to the U.S. business unless the maintenance of the investments is the principal activity of the business.

Foreign Earned Income and Housing Exclusion

A qualifying U.S. citizen or resident who works abroad may elect to exclude from gross income up to $80,000 (for calendar year 2005 and 2006) of foreign "earned income" attributable to a period of residence in a foreign country. In addition, the qualifying individual may elect to exclude from gross income a certain amount of employer-provided housing costs.

For this purpose, foreign earned income includes wages, salaries, or professional fees, and other amounts received as compensation for personal services actually rendered when the taxpayer's tax home was located in a foreign country and they establish their qualified residence in the foreign country. In cases when a taxpayer is engaged in a trade or business in which both personal services and capital are material income-producing factors, a reasonable allowance as compensation for the personal services, not in excess of 30 percent of the share of the net profits of the trade or business, is considered as earned income.

Tax home. Generally, an individual's tax home is either their regular or principal place of business or, if no principal place of business exists, their regular and principal place of abode. However, an individual is not considered to have a tax home in a foreign country for any period during which their abode is in the United States. Temporary presence or maintenance of a dwelling in the U.S. does not necessarily mean that an abode is in the U.S. during that time

Residence test. To establish a qualified residence in a foreign country, an individual must satisfy either the bona fide resident test or the physical presence test. A U.S. citizen is a bona fide resident of a foreign country if he or she resides there for an uninterrupted period that includes a full tax year. The person may leave the country for brief or temporary trips for vacation or business and still meet the test. Once the bona fide residence test is met, the foreign earning income exclusion or the foreign housing costs exclusion is available for any partial tax year in which the period began or ended.

 Example Joseph Baker is sent by his employer to Lisbon, Portugal, as a corporate representative. Baker arrives in Lisbon with his family on November 1, 2004. His assignment is indefinite, and he intends to live there with his family until he is transferred to a new post. He immediately

establishes residence in Lisbon. On April 1, 2005, Baker arrives in the United States to meet with officers at the corporate home office, leaving his family in Lisbon. He returns to Lisbon on May 1 and continues living there. On January 1, 2006, he has completed an uninterrupted period or residence for a full tax year (2005) and may therefore qualify as a bona fide resident of Portugal.

A U.S. citizen or resident alien meets the physical presence test if he or she spends 330 full days out of any 12 consecutive month period in a foreign country (or countries). The 12-month period may begin on any day of the year. The period ends with the day before the corresponding calendar day in the 12th succeeding month. It is not necessary to begin or end any 12-month period with the first full day after arrival in a foreign country or the last full day before departure. Also, one 12-month period may overlap another.

 Example Michael Trimble is physically present in a foreign country from January 1, 2005, through June 30, 2006, and has $110,000 of foreign earned income for 2005 and $60,000 of foreign earned income for the first six months in 2006. For 2005, Trimble excludes $80,000, the annual exclusion, since he was abroad for the entire year. For 2006, he excludes $47,343 (216/365 of the $80,000 annual exclusion for 2006), since only 216 days of 2006 are included within a consecutive 12-month period in which he is in the foreign country for 330 days. The number of days (216) is determined by counting back 330 days (to August 5, 2005) from the last full day he was in the foreign country (June 30, 2006). Thus, the consecutive 12-month period including those 330 days begins on August 5, 2005, and ends on August 4, 2006. The number of days in 2006 falling in that 12-month period is 216.

 Planning Alert If an individual who makes his tax home in a foreign country is required to leave the foreign country because of war, civil unrest, or other adverse conditions, then he or she is excepted from both the bona fide residence and the physical presence test requirements.

Foreign housing costs. An individual must meet the tax home and qualified residency requirements to exclude foreign housing costs. For this purpose, employer-provided foreign housing costs are amounts that would be included in the salary of the individual, as well as any reimbursements. A number of calculations are required to keep the foreign housing exclusion in line with the foreign income exclusion limits. A self-employed individual is entitled to deduct from gross income a certain amount of foreign housing expenses in lieu of the exclusion.

Making the Move Abroad

If you are in the position to be making the move abroad, either on a temporary or permanent basis, the following checklist provides some important topics to consider before making the move.

Starting tax residence in your new "home" country:
- How does the country levy taxes?
- What are the rules for determining resident status?
- Are there any applicable residence or tax treaties?
- How are expatriate employees treated?
- How are immigrants treated?

Tax treatment of residents and nonresidents:
- How is tax liability determined?
- What are the income tax rates?
- How are taxes paid ?
- Does source of income matter?
- What tax credits and deductions are available?
- Are there any local taxes imposed?
- Are any estate, gift and wealth taxes imposed?
- How are pensions and other retirement pay treated?
- What about health and social security benefits?

Inbound tax issues:
- Can you accelerate or defer timing of residency?
- Can you split income across tax years and countries?
- Did you realize income and capital gains prior to residence?
- Did you transfer assets prior to residence?
- Are there any tax treaty issues for nonresidents?

Ending residence in your former "home" country:
- What factors determine end of residence?
- How do you sever other tax ties?
- Are there any income tax and capital gains tax considerations?
- Are there any tax-related departure requirements?

Tax treatment of residents working abroad:

- Do you have any income tax liability?
- Will you qualify for foreign tax credit or treaty relief?
- What happens to your pension or retirement pay?
- What about health and social security benefits?
- Does your employer offer a salary package?

Appendix A—Tax Planning Checklist

Do you have or expect-

❑ A change in marital status? (See page 95)

❑ A major change in your income level? (See page 11)

❑ Children? (See page 91)

❑ Education expenses? (See page 97)

❑ Alternative minimum tax liability? (See pages 34 and 134)

❑ Estimated taxes? (See pages 107 and 134)

❑ To start a new business? (See page 111)

Do you have (or could you have) income of the following types-

❑ Self-employment income for which you control billing and collection? (See pages 19, 21 and 134)

❑ Deferred compensation arrangement with your employer? (See pages 19 and 70)

❑ A year-end bonus? (See page 21)

❑ Incentive stock options? (See page 22)

❑ Interest? (See page 19)

❑ Dividends? (See pages 22 and 47)

❑ Annuities? (See page 19)

❑ IRAs? (See pages 22 and 61)

❑ Capital gains or losses? (See pages 22 and 43)

❑ Social security? (See pages 17, 73 and 134)

❑ Lump-sum distribution from profit-sharing plan? (See page 63)

Do you have (or could you have) deductions of the following types-

❑ Employee-related expenses? (See page 31)

❑ Medical expenses? (See pages 32 and 119)

❑ Charitable contributions? (See page 36)

❑ Bad debts? (See page 37)

❑ Depreciation? (See page 38)

❏ Expenses related to vacation home? (See pages 41 and 60)

❏ Automobile expenses? (See page 122)

❏ Travel and entertainment? (See page 125)

Do you own investments of the following type-

❏ Capital assets? (See page 43)

❏ Inherited property? (See page 50)

❏ Shares of mutual funds? (See pages 51 and 54)

❏ A small business? (See page 55)

❏ Tax-exempt bonds? (See pages 22, 57 and 104)

❏ A principal residence? (See page 58)

Will you receive retirement benefits from any of the following-

❏ A traditional or Roth IRA? (See pages 22 and 61)

❏ An employer-sponsored plan? (See page 70)

❏ A retirement plan for self-employed persons? (See pages 69 and 131)

❏ Social security? (See pages 17, 73 and 134)

Have you planned for any of the following retirement expenses-

❏ Estimated tax liability? (See pages 77 and 107)

❏ Medical benefits? (See page 77)

❏ Long-term health care? (See page 80)

❏ Incapacity? (See page 81)

❏ Housing? (See page 82)

Have you taken any steps to minimize any estate tax liability-

❏ Marital deduction trust? (See page 84)

❏ Lifetime gift exclusion? (See page 84)

❏ Annual gift tax exclusion? (See page 85)

❏ Education or medical expense exclusion? (See page 85)

Do you have any tax strategies involving your family-

❏ Shifted income to your kids? (See page 91)

❏ Protected dependency exemptions? (See page 92)

❏   Claimed child tax credit? (See page 95)

❏   Claimed child and dependent care credit? (See page 96)

Have you considered how to pay for your kids' education-

❏   Education tax credits? (See page 97)

❏   Coverdell education savings account? (See page 99)

❏   Early withdrawal from an IRA? (See page 100)

❏   Education loan interest deduction? (See page 101)

❏   Deduction for higher education expenses? (See page 101)

❏   Qualified tuition program? (See page 102)

❏   Employer's educational assistance plan? (See page 104)

❏   U.S. savings bond? (See pages 22, 57 and 104)

Have you considered the following tax issues in starting a business-

❏   Choosing the business form? (See page 111)

❏   Accounting period or method? (See page 115)

❏   Start-up costs? (See page 116)

❏   Retirement planning? (See pages 117 and 131)

❏   Employing family members? (See page 118)

If you are (or plan on being) self-employed, have you considered-

❏   Medical insurance? (See page 119)

❏   Buying or leasing an automobile? (See page 122)

❏   Substantiating your expenses? (See page 125)

❏   Home office? (See page 128)

❏   A retirement plan? (See pages 69 and 131)

❏   Self-employment tax? (See page 134)

❏   Alternative minimum tax? (See pages 34 and 134)

❏   Worker status? (See page 135)

Appendix B
Tax Calendar

Here is a calendar of important tax dates for year-end 2005 and 2006 that will be useful if you figure your taxes on a calendar-year basis.

Year-End 2005

August 15	Individual income tax return for 2004 is due if you were granted an automatic extension of the April 15 deadline.
September 15	Third installment of 2005 estimated tax is due.
October 17	Individual income tax return for 2004 is due if you were granted a second extension of the filing deadline. This is the final deadline.
December 31	Marital status on this date determines 2005 filing status.

2006

January 17	Your final payment of 2005 estimated tax is due unless you file your 2005 income tax return by January 31 and pay the full balance of tax due.
April 17	Individual income tax return for 2005 is due with payment of any tax due. If an extension is required, file your request by this date. Last day for making your 2005 IRA contribution.
	First installment of 2006 estimated tax is due.
June 15	Second installment of 2006 estimated tax is due.
August 15	Individual income tax return for 2005 is due if you were granted an automatic extension of the April 17 deadline.
September 15	Third installment of 2006 estimated tax is due.
October 16	Individual income tax return for 2005 is due if you were granted a second extension of the filing deadline. This is the final deadline.
December 15	Wrap up year-end transactions.
December 31	Marital status on this date determines 2006 filing status.

Appendix C—Income Tax Rates

2005 Tax Rate Schedules

	If taxable income is over-	But not over-	The tax is:	of the amount over-
Single—	$0	$7,300	$0 + 10%	$0
Schedule X	7,300	29,700	730.00 + 15%	7,300
	29,700	71,950	4,090.00 + 25%	29,700
	71,950	150,150	14,652.50 + 28%	71,950
	150,150	326,450	36,548.50 + 33%	150,150
	326,450	....	94,727.50 + 35%	326,450
Married filing	$0	$14,600	$0 + 10%	$0
jointly or	14,600	59,400	1,460.00 + 15%	14,600
Qualifying	59,400	119,950	8,180.00 + 25%	59,400
Widow(er)—	119,950	182,800	23,317.50 + 28%	119,950
Schedule Y-1	182,800	326,450	40,915.50 + 33%	182,800
	326,450	....	88,320.00 + 35%	326,450
Head of	$0	$10,450	$0 + 10%	$0
Household—	10,450	39,800	1,045.00 + 15%	10,450
Schedule Z	39,800	102,800	5,447.50 + 25%	39,800
	102,800	166,450	21,197.50 + 28%	102,800
	166,450	326,450	39,019.50 + 33%	166,450
	326,450	....	91,819.50 + 35%	326,450
Married filing	$0	$7,300	$0 + 10%	$0
separately—	7,300	29,700	730.00 + 15%	7,300
Schedule Y-2	29,700	59,975	4,090.00 + 25%	29,700
	59,975	91,400	11,658.75 + 28%	59,975
	91,400	163,225	20,457.75 + 33%	91,400
	163,225	....	44,160.00 + 35%	163,225

Estates and Nongrantor Trusts

If taxable income is over–	But not over–	The tax is–	of the amount over–
$0	$2,000	$0 + 15%	$0
2,000	4,700	300.00 + 25%	2,000
4,700	7,150	975.00 + 28%	4,700
7,150	9,750	1,661.00 + 33%	7,150
9,750	....	2,519.00 + 35%	9,750

Corporations

If taxable income is over–	But not over–	The tax is–	of the amount over–
$0	$50,000	$0 + 15%	$0
50,000	75,000	7,500 + 25%	50,000
75,000	100,000	13,750 + 34%	75,000
100,000	335,000	22,250 + 39%	100,000
335,000	10,000,000	113,900 + 34%	335,000
10,000,000	15,000,000	3,400,000 + 35%	10,000,000
15,000,000	18,333,333	5,150,000 + 38%	15,000,000
18,333,333	....	35%	0

Appendix D—Average Itemized Deduction Chart

Preliminary Average Itemized Deductions
for 2003 Returns by Adjusted Gross Income Ranges

Adjusted Gross Income Ranges	Medical Expenses	Taxes	Interest	Contributions
Under $15,000	$ 7,818	$ 2,459	$6,834	$1,443
$15,000 to $30,000	6,382	2,442	6,844	2,020
$30,000 to $50,000	5,355	3,332	6,979	2,066
$50,000 to $100,000	5,651	5,464	8,448	2,666
$100,000 to $200,000	10,515	10,042	11,350	4,000
$200,000+	25,719	36,354	20,381	18,011

Appendix E—Deductions Checklist

Deductions for Business or Profession

Accounting, engineering and
legal fees

Advertising

Bad debts

Banking charges—interest paid,
safe deposit boxes, etc.

Business and professional
books, journals, reports

Car, truck, or other vehicle
business expenses

Casualty losses (storm, fire, etc.)

Charitable contributions

Conventions, cost of attending

Depreciable assets (car, furniture, fixtures, etc.) acquired
for employee's use

Domestic production activities

Education expense (travel,
tuition, etc.) to maintain or

improve skills required in
the trade or business

Employee Expenses
- Employment related
  insurance
- Professional fees, dues,
  licenses, etc.
- Tools
- Uniforms

Freight charges

Health insurance, personal
(100% if self-employed)

Insurance on business
property

Meal and lodging expenses

Moving expenses

Office Expenses
- Janitor service
- Postage

- Rent for office
- Security (night watch
  service, etc.)
- Stationery—letter heads,
  cards, etc.
- Utilities (lights, telephone,
  water, garbage, etc)

Repairs and maintenance of
business property

Research and experimental
expenditures

Salaries, wages, commis-
sions, bonuses, etc., paid

Taxes and costs of preparing
returns

Theft losses, not compen-
sated by insurance

Travel and entertainment
expenses

"Personal" Deductions on Schedule A (Form 1040)

Deductible Only if Deductions are Itemized:

Amortizable premiums on
taxable bonds

Appraisal fees (2% floor)

Casualty and theft losses—
business property (2% floor)

Casualty and theft losses—
nonbusiness property

Charitable contributions

Clerical help and office rent
(2% floor)

Depreciation on home com-
puter (2% floor)

Excess deductions on an
estate (2% floor)

Expenses in earning taxable
income (2% floor)

Fees to collect interest and
dividends (2% floor)

Gambling losses—limited to
winnings

Hobby expenses to the extent
of income (2% floor)

Impairment-related work
expenses

Indirect deductions of pass-
through entities (2% floor)

Interest Expense
- Home mortgage interest
- Investment interest (limited)
- Student loan interest
  (limited, but not
  itemized)

Investment fees and expenses
(2% floor)

IRA fees (2% floor)

Legal expenses—nonbusiness
(2% floor)

Loss on deposits (2% floor)

Medical, dental, hospital
expenses (7.5% floor)

Repayments of income (2%
floor)

Repayments of social security
benefits (2% floor)

Repayments under claim of
right

Safe deposit box rent (2%
floor)

Service charges on dividend reinvestment plans (2% floor)

Taxes, nonbusiness, non-rental, non-royalty:

- Advice, preparation, legal fees (2% floor)
- Cooperative housing taxes (share)
- Estate taxes on income in respect of decedent
- Foreign income and real property taxes paid
- State and local income or general sales taxes paid
- Personal property, and real property taxes paid

Taxes, other

- Taxes on property produc-

ing rent or royalties

Unrecovered investment in an annuity

Unreimbursed employee expenses (2% floor)

- Business bad debt
- Business liability insurance
- Damages for breach of employment contract
- Depreciation on computers and cellphones
- Dues to professional societies or chamber of commerce
- Education related to work
- Home office
- Job search expenses
- Legal fees

- Licenses and regulatory fees
- Occupational taxes
- Repayment of income aid payment
- Research expenses of a college professor
- Subscriptions to professional journals and trade magazines related to work
- Summer school expense of teachers
- Tools used in work
- Travel, Transportation, Meals, Lodging, and Gifts
- Union dues and expenses
- Work clothes and uniforms

"Personal"-Type Items Which are Not Deductible

Adoption expenses (however, tax credit allowable)

Campaign expenses

Capital expenditures

Club dues or fees

Depreciable assets held for personal use

Expenses of earning tax-exempt income

Expenses of attending stockholders meeting

Fees or licenses (personal)

Fines or penalties for violating of the law

Funeral or burial expenses

Gifts to individuals

Hobby losses

Home repair and maintenance

Insurance premiums (life, disability, home, etc.)

Legal fees (personal)

Personal living or family expenses including:

- Automobile upkeep

- Domestic servants (except as child care)
- Home rental
- Home utilities
- Losses from sale of personal property, home
- Travel expenses (commuting, vacation)

Professional accreditation fees

Training or special courses used to obtain employment position

Appendix F—Tax Items Affected by AGI

Adjusted gross income (AGI) levels in excess of certain phaseout thresholds limit the following deductions, credits and other tax benefits. This chart provides the beginning point for the 2005 thresholds and the ending point of the phaseout (where applicable).

Tax Item	Taxpayers Affected	Phaseout—Begin	Phaseout—End
Itemized Deductions (Overall Limit)	single, head of household, joint filers	$145,950	phaseout varies by taxpayer
	married filing separate	$72,975	phaseout varies by taxpayer
7.5% Floor on Medical Deductions	those itemizing medical expenses	7.5% of AGI	N/A
2% Floor on Misc. Itemized Deductions	those itemizing misc. expenses	2% of AGI	N/A
10% Floor on Casualty Loss	those itemizing casualty losses	10% of AGI	N/A
Personal Exemption	single	$145,950	$268,450
	head of household	$182,450	$304,950
	joint filers	$218,950	$341,450
	married filing separate	$109,475	$170,725
Child Tax Credit	single, head of household	$75,000	phaseout varies by taxpayer
	married filing separate	$55,000	phaseout varies by taxpayer
	joint filers	$110,000	phaseout varies by taxpayer
Dependent Care Credit	joint filers, head of household, single	35% credit if AGI not over $15,000	20% credit if AGI over $43,000
Elderly and Disabled Credit	single, head of household	$7,500	$17,500
	joint filers	$10,000	$25,000
	married filing separate	$5,000	$12,500
Adoption Credit	all filers	$159,450	$199,450
Earned Income Credit	no child, single, head of household	$6,530	$11,750
	no child, joint filers	$8,530	$13,750
	one child, single, head of household	$14,370	$31,030

Tax Item	Taxpayers Affected	Phaseout—Begin	Phaseout—End
	one child, joint filers	$16,370	$33,030
	two or more children, single, head of household	$14,370	$35,263
	two or more children, joint filers	$16,370	$37,263
HOPE Credit	single, head of household	$43,000	$53,000
	joint filers	$87,000	$107,000
Lifetime Learning Credit	single, head of household	$43,000	$53,000
	joint filers	$87,000	$107,000
Student Loan Interest Deduction	single, head of household	$50,000	$65,000
	joint filers	$105,000	$135,000
Savings Bonds Interest Exclusion	single, head of household	$61,200	$76,200
	joint filers	$91,850	$121,850
Coverdell Education Accounts	single, head of household, married filing separate	$95,000	$110,000
	joint filers	$190,000	$220,000
IRA Deduction	single, head of household	$50,000	$60,000
	joint filers	$70,000	$80,000
	married filing separate	$0	$10,000
Roth IRA Eligibility	single, head of household	$95,000	$110,000
	joint filers	$150,000	$160,000
	married filing separate	$0	$10,000
First-time DC Homebuyer	single, head of household, married filing separate	$70,000	$90,000
	joint filers	$110,000	$130,000
Rental Real Estate Passive Losses	single, joint filers, head of household	$100,000	$150,000
	married filing separate	$50,000	$75,000
Mortgage Bond Subsidy Recapture	all filers	AGI relative to area median income	N/A

INDEX

Accounting methods
cash method 18; 113
accrual method 113
Adoption expenses 93
Alternative minimum tax
capital gains 51
incentive stock options 23
liability 11; 51
multi-year planning 34
preference items 11
Annuities 19
Automobiles
buy vs. lease 121
depreciation caps 122
standard mileage vs. actual costs 122
substantiation of expenses 124
Average itemized deductions 153
Bad debts 37
Bonds
I savings bonds 17
tax-exempt 57
TIPS 15
zero-coupon 15
Bonuses 21
Business planning
accounting methods 113
C corporation 110
choice of business entity 109
limited liability company 110
partnerships 109
S corporation 110
sole proprietorships 109
start-up costs 114
Capital gains
collectibles 50
dividends 47
gifts 49
holding periods 44
inherited property 50
qualified small business stock 55
mutual funds 54

rates 43
sale of principal residence 58
specialized small business investment company 56
wash sales 53
Charitable contributions 36
Checklist, tax planning 147
Child and dependent care credit 95
Child tax credit 94
Code Sec. 179 expensing 40; 123
Collectibles
capital gains rate 50
Deductions checklist 154
Deferred income
strategies 18
retirement plans 61
Dependents
child tax credit 94
child and dependent care credit 95
divorced parents 93
exemptions 90
multiple support agreements 92
Depreciation
Code Sec. 179 expensing 40; 123
MACRS 38
vehicles 122
Dividends 47
Education
Coverdell savings accounts 98
employer education assistance exclusion 102
IRA withdrawals 99
higher education expense deduction 100
hope and lifetime learning credit 96
qualified tuition programs 101
savings bond interest exclusion 57; 103
student loan interest 99
Employees
family employment 89; 116
itemized deductions 28
spending accounts 22
Entertainment and meal expenses 127
Estate planning
educational or medical expense exclusion 85
estate tax exclusion 83

generation-skipping transfer tax 88
gift tax exclusion 85
marital deduction 84
rates 86
state death taxes 88
stepped-up basis 86

Estimated tax
payment rules 105
safe harbors 106

Filing status
marriage penalty 94
standard deduction 28
tax rates 10

Flexible spending accounts 21; 119

401(k) plans
catch-up contributions 67
hardship distributions 70
maximum contributions 67
participation in 67
self-employed individuals 69

Gifts
capital gains 49
gift tax 83
educational expenses 85
medical expenses 85

Hobbies
business v. hobby 38

Home office deduction 41; 128
I bonds 17

Incentive stock options 19; 23

Income
accelerating 21
deferring 18
exclusions 16
taxable income inclusions 15
independent contractor 134

Individual retirement accounts (IRAs)
catch-up contributions 64
distributions, medical 34
education IRAs (Coverdell education savings accounts) 98
establishment of 64; 132
rollovers 68
Roth IRAs 66
unemployed spouse 66

Installment sales 20

Interest
income 19
points.. 41
student loans 99

International tax
foreign income 141
housing exclusion... 143
income exclusion 143
sourcing rules 140
U.S. jurisdiction 139

Investments
capital gains... 43
dividends... 47
holding periods 44
tax-exempt bonds.. 57
wash sales 53

Itemized deductions
average 153
bunching 30
income limits... 27
miscellaneous itemized deductions 31
statutory employees.. 31

Keogh plans 69; 131

Kiddie tax
avoiding 89
mechanics.. 89

Like-kind exchanges 20

Long-term care insurance 33; 80

Loans
interest on student loans.. 99
retirement plans 70

Lump sum distributions 63

Marriage penalty 94

Meal and entertainment expenses 127

Medical expenses
Health savings accounts (HSAs)...............................34; 119
IRA withdrawals.. 34
itemized deductions.. 28
long-term care insurance 33; 80
Medical savings accounts (MSAs)................................ 118
self-employed.. 117

Moving expense deduction 125

Mutual funds 54

Power of attorney 80

Residences
exclusion of gain on sale 58
seller-paid points 41

Retirement plans and planning
early retirement, planning for 75
early withdrawals 62
employer-sponsored plans 69
five-year averaging 63
incapacity 81
IRAs 64
Keogh plans 69; 131
lump-sum distributions 63
rollovers 68
Roth IRAs 66
Social Security 72
revocable trusts 81

Roth IRAs
establishment of 66
rollovers to 68

Self-employed
automobiles 121
computers 130
health savings accounts 119
home office 128
meal expenses 127
medical expenses 117
medical savings accounts 118
office equipment 129
self-employment tax 133
retirement plans 130
travel and entertainment 125
worker status 134

Self-employment tax 133

SIMPLE plans 132

Simplified employee pensions (SEPs) 130

Social security
estimate of benefits 73
retirement age 72
taxation of benefits 17

Standard deduction 28

Tax-exempt bonds
yields 57

Tax calendar 150

Tax planning checklist 147

Tax rate reduction credit 12

Tax rate schedules 151

Travel expenses 126

Treasury Inflation Protected Securities (TIPS) 15

Vacation home 41; 60

Wash sales 53

Quick Tax Facts—Key Tax Figures

10-Year Tax Forecast

The chart below provides important amounts and percentages for 2002 through 2011. Additional limitations, inflation adjustments, effective dates and transitional rules may apply.

	2002	2003	2004	2005	2006	2007	2008	2009	2010	2011
CAPITAL GAINS										
Capital gains rate	20%	15%*	15%	15%	15%	15%	15%	20%	20%	20%
Capital gains rate for taxpayers in 10% or 15% bracket	10%	5%*	5%	5%	5%	5%	0%	10%	10%	10%
DIVIDENDS										
Dividends rate (taxed as capital gains)	Did not apply	15%	15%	15%	15%	15%	15%	Will not apply	Will not apply	Will not apply
Dividends rate for taxpayers in 10% or 15% bracket (taxed as capital gains)	Did not apply	5%	5%	5%	5%	5%	0%	Will not apply	Will not apply	Will not apply
INCOME TAX RATE REDUCTIONS										
Top bracket	38.6%	35%	35%	35%	35%	35%	35%	35%	35%	39.6%
Fifth bracket	35%	33%	33%	33%	33%	33%	33%	33%	33%	36%
Fourth bracket	30%	28%	28%	28%	28%	28%	28%	28%	28%	31%
Third bracket	27%	25%	25%	25%	25%	25%	25%	25%	25%	28%
Second bracket	15%	15%	15%	15%	15%	15%	15%	15%	15%	15%
Initial bracket	10%	10%	10%	10%	10%	10%	10%	10%	10%	No 10% bracket

*post-5/5/03

10-Year Tax Forecast

	2002	2003	2004	2005	2006	2007	2008	2009	2010	2011
EXPANSION OF 10% BRACKET										
Taxable income limit—joint filers	$12,000	$14,000	$14,000*	$14,000*	$14,000*	$14,000*	$14,000*	$14,000*	$14,000*	No 10% bracket
Taxable income limit—single filers	$6,000	$7,000	$7,000*	$7,000*	$7,000*	$7,000*	$7,000*	$7,000*	$7,000*	No 10% bracket
MARRIAGE PENALTY RELIEF										
Basic standard deduction for joint filers—Percentage of single filer amount	Did not apply	200%	200%	200%	200%	200%	200%	200%	200%	Will not apply
15% bracket size for joint filers—Percentage of 15% bracket size for single filers	Did not apply	200%	200%	200%	200%	200%	200%	200%	200%	Will not apply
CHILD TAX CREDIT										
Amount per child	$600	$1,000	$1,000	$1,000	$1,000	$1,000	$1,000	$1,000	$1,000	$500
AMT EXEMPTION										
Joint filers	$49,000	$58,000	$58,000	$58,000	$45,000	$45,000	$45,000	$45,000	$45,000	$45,000
Single filers	$35,750	$40,250	$40,250	$40,250	$33,750	$33,750	$33,750	$33,750	$33,750	$33,750
CODE SEC. 179 EXPENSING										
Deduction amount	$24,000	$100,000	$100,000*	$100,000*	$100,000*	$100,000*	$25,000	$25,000	$25,000	$25,000
Investment limitation (on cost of property)	$200,000	$400,000	$400,000*	$400,000*	$400,000*	$400,000*	$200,000	$200,000	$200,000	$200,000

* before adjustment for inflation